TURN UP THE MUSIC

TURN UP THE MUSIC

✦

Prevention Strategies to Help Parents Through the Rap, Rock, Pop and Metal Years

*For Parents, Educators
and Other Adults
Who Care About Kids*

Jeff Dess, M.A., MAC, CP4

iUniverse, Inc.
New York Lincoln Shanghai

TURN UP THE MUSIC
Prevention Strategies to Help Parents Through the Rap, Rock, Pop and Metal Years

iUniverse books may be ordered through booksellers or by contacting:

iUniverse
2021 Pine Lake Road, Suite 100
Lincoln, NE 68512
www.iuniverse.com
1-800-Authors (1-800-288-4677)

Contact Information:
Tune-In Inc at (678)455-2860
E-Mail address is
tunein123@earthlink.net

ISBN-13: 978-0-595-31220-7 (pbk)
ISBN-13: 978-0-595-76042-8 (ebk)
ISBN-10: 0-595-31220-9 (pbk)
ISBN-10: 0-595-76042-2 (ebk)

Printed in the United States of America

To my parents,

who always believed in me when others did not,

and who helped me believe in myself

To my wife, a gifted teacher,

mother and wife, who encourages and supports what I do

And to Ian and Adam, who help me understand

what is really important each and every day

Contents

Acknowledgments

It is difficult to acknowledge the many people throughout my life who have helped me get to this point. I would be remiss if I didn't acknowledge my two sisters, Candy and Carla, who have always been understanding and supportive, as well as people like Tim, Beverly and Bill Yedor, who provided much-needed support while I was growing up. I also thank John Bailey, who gave me my start and allowed someone very green to step into a position ahead of much more experienced people, and Dr. Miller, my high school principal, without whose help and encouragement I would not have been admitted to college. To the Simunek family, Jim, Mason, Paige and Candy, for all their support and encouragement through the years. To my colleagues, with whom I have worked with for so many years and who have developed into an extended family of sorts—Patti Agatston, Wendy Arrecis, Mike Carpenter, Jeff Inman, Luisa Resendiz, Paula Sue Barbian, Janice Mosher, Joyce Hutchings, Jane Camp and a special thanks to Liz Bozzuto who encouraged me to enter into the field of prevention. Thanks also to colleagues, Rick Beal, Linda Stone, Sundra Davis, and Alyse Cooper Pribish who were part of the PI Center for some time. We have developed into one of the best prevention programs in the nation, and I am very proud of the prevention work we do for adults and youth alike. Thank you to all of the therapists in the community who support what we do. We could not do it with out you. (The Prevention Intervention Center received a National award for Student Assistance Program of Excellence in the year 2002).

Thanks to all the principals of Area Four and other administrators and superintendents who have supported what I do, allowing me to attend their meetings and entrusting me with the responsibility of doing what's best for kids. I have learned from each and every one of you. Thanks also to Debbie and Richard Miller, Sharon Lightstone, Briane and Mark Myers, Barbara Jones, Lillian Lurye, Merrilee Heflin, and Janet Hosler, all of whom have provided feedback and ideas by reading early drafts of the book or encouraging me to write it in the first place, not only for the support and insight but also for their friendship. I thank all the wonderful teachers, counselors, and other educators too numerous to mention individually, who have impacted my life in so many different ways. If only all adults had the opportunity to see the magic you create each and every day, they would surely be amazed.

I would like to thank Judy Barrif, who had a passion for working with her clients, a passion for life and was a good friend (*"Make yourself a good day."*) and to Chris for the interview and the added insight. Thanks go to Joe Gandolfo for his encouragement, to Angela Carter for listening, to Suzie Brookshire and Barbara Hancock for their words of wisdom, to Eric for the "drug-free party" note in my mailbox, and to Teresa for the kind words. I also acknowledge Pastor Jeff Vermilya and Rabbi Steven Lebow (about as far right and left as two people could be) for their insight. To the hundreds of speakers I have listened to through the years who have ignited my creativity, thank you. Thanks also to the ECCC and other PTA members (who seem to work 24\7) without whose support I could not do what I do, and to Cathy Finck, Jean Bannister and Bonnie Brand, (Underage Drinking Task Force) worker bees with an unbelievable amount of energy and passion. I also want to thank the thousands of parents I have had the pleasure of talking to and working with over the years, and the thousands of kids who have taught me more than I could ever teach them. I would like to thank my editors for their patience, support and encouragement—Gail Tyson, who challenged me to rethink my ideas again and again and who read with such a critical eye, and Melanie Smallie, who believed in my ideas, saw potential in my work and whose positive energy was contagious. I could not have done this without you. Finally, I would like to thank my friends Mike Madden, John Brennan, Paul Schultz, Greg and Mark Johnson, Randy Lane, Mike Pfeiffer and Jerry Lawrence (we miss you) for allowing me the opportunity to share my love of music with them all these years, and to the musicians who have enriched my life and continue to do so, thank you.

Foreword

By *Cathy Finck*

I am an ordinary mother of two extraordinary adult children; Robin Finck, former guitar player for Nine Inch Nails, currently with Guns N Roses, and Jamie Finck, Southwest Airlines flight attendant and DJ. I say with candor and complete conviction that had *Turn Up the Music* been available while my husband and I were parenting our growing children, my progress as a successful Mom would have been faster.

I believe if parents and families will utilize the ideas and techniques offered in this book, the heartfelt experiences of other people and the author's insight, they will find practical ways to grow healthy children and healthy families. What's the big deal about music, media and children? I found my answer to that question through my own reaction to the music and media my children were exposed to, and from sharing in my son's experience as a rock musician and my daughter's experience as a DJ. I learned that no two people see or hear a piece of music or media the same way. I learned that talking about my values was more important than I realized and necessary to counteract the embedded values and points of view that existed in the music and media my children were consuming. I almost missed a great opportunity in my life as a Mom—to learn about my children's developing values and points of view and how I could compete with music and media to influence them. I am still amazed to this day at how apparent it is to me now (but was not then), the role music and media played in their decision making as adolescents and in shaping their values, and mine. That's precisely why I believe this book is so important for parents, children and families!

I know you can help influence your child's values and prevent your child from buying into some of the dangerous messages in today's music and media culture. I also know you cannot prevent what you do not acknowledge and understand. Believe me, you will be enlightened and informed when you listen to your kids' music—you may also be dismayed, alarmed and frightened. But take heart and keep watching and listening, courageous parenting is not for the faint of heart yet it is the single greatest gift we can give our children and ourselves. To be courageous you need only to give more energy to loving and parenting your children than you give to what you fear for your children.

In *Turn Up The Music*, author Jeff Dess simply and brilliantly provides useful prevention strategies to help parents help their kids through the Rap, Rock, Pop and Metal (and media saturated) years of their children's adolescence. I sincerely hope you will take this encouragement and implement some of the strategies offered in this book. If you do, you will be afforded the opportunity to share your values and perspective with your kids (not criticize theirs). This will help them interpret the music and media they are overexposed to and can help them dodge the dangers that lurk around every corner of their adolescent passage.

Here's to a safe journey through adolescence, for all courageous parents, educators and children alike. Read on, and please parents—*Turn Up The Music*!

Introduction

"We are only immortal for a limited time."

Neil Peart of Rush

I love what I do, but there are times I wish I didn't have to do it, or didn't have to talk about it. I wish I didn't have to walk into a school and provide crisis response and grief counseling for the kids, parents, and faculty who just lost a friend, student, son or daughter, or sibling to suicide. I wish I didn't have to talk to a child who doesn't want to go to school any more because he or she is being bullied. I wish the things kids are taught in kindergarten—to use their words and not their fists—would stick with them throughout their lives, and that parents would support that. I wish kids didn't feel that they have to join gangs to replace whatever they feel is missing in their lives. I wish that all those children who signed "*I will not use drugs*" contracts in 4th and 5th grade would agree to sign another one in 8th, 10th, and 12th grade, and believe in what they were pledging. I wish adults would stop putting academic pressure on kids to succeed at four and five years old, and would revisit the concept of teaching the whole child. I wish we would allow our kids time to play. **I wish parents would consider alcohol a drug.** I know you have wishes, too. I'm sure there are many things in your profession—whether your work is that of a homemaker or attorney—that you wish you did not have to do, or at least not repeat over and over again. Prevention is all about increasing the odds that your child will grow up healthy and drug-free. Prevention is being proactive in one's efforts, in creating strategies to address a variety of issues, challenges and concerns before they become out-of-control and require intervention. Prevention is about building relationships. We all are responsible for prevention.

When prevention initiatives began, prevention specialists thought that information alone could change behavior. In some people it can, but in most people, information alone is not enough. How many of you exercise, eat chicken and fish more than red meat, get eight hours of sleep a night, find 20 minutes a day for yourself, and have eliminated most sweets and processed foods? Most of us have access to all kinds of health information. Most of us believe that if we followed these guidelines, we'd be healthier, so why don't we follow them? **We need more than just information.** People must learn skills to go along with the information they receive, and those skills must be practiced over and over again. It's the same for young people. Knowing who should be responsible for teaching kids pro-social skills is still up for debate. Most parents would say that they teach their children the social and life skills they need to be successful in life, with the school's role being to reinforce and support the parents. I agree. I wish all parents were doing just that. But the truth is we're not.

This book introduces parents to prevention strategies that use music as the catalyst for conversation. It is important for parents to understand how artists and musicians send our kids messages every day that we as adults tend to ignore or disregard as fabrication or hype. We must understand the role that music and the media play in many of our kids' and teenagers' lives, just like it did in ours when we were growing up. I chose topics and genres of music to talk about based on my experience in working with youth and teens for the last 20-plus years. Some of the chapters in this book use music to introduce the topic, while other chapters talk directly about a particular genre of music and its impact—both positive and negative—on its listener. The book is full of prevention strategies that cover a variety of topics relating to kids and teens between 4th and 12th grades.

Some material you may find offensive, which is why it is rated somewhere between PG-13 and R. My intention is not to offend anyone, but in talking passionately about important issues, it can happen. I would rather have this discussion with you than sweep it under the rug. There are many strategies and ideas offered throughout the book that are specifically geared to youth and teens. You decide which of these you would like to share with your child. There also is a chapter included for educators, in the hope that we can all gain a better perspective on the importance of working together to raise healthy drug-free kids.

From one passionate person to another, it's time to begin our conversation. Let's rock.

"If It's Too Loud, You're Too Old."
(Written on the back of a Kiss T-shirt during the mid-70s)

Whoever coined the phrase "sex, drugs, and rock 'n roll" got it partly right. In those days, adolescents had their share of buzzwords—just not quite in that order. I went to high school in the early 70s, and for many of us, music became the catalyst for all things to follow. Music was the first thing to be turned on when we got into a car. For many of my friends, the sound system became the most important piece of equipment, and whatever music we played became an autobiography of sorts. Whether the music was metal, rock, soul, or pop, we hoped someone sitting in the car next to us would hear it and think, "*Wow, how cool are they?*" Of course, if the other car was filled with adults, we would turn the music up just a little bit louder, to see if we could get a reaction. We defined ourselves by the music we listened to.

Our image in part was made up of musical ingredients, along with the sports we played and the grades we got, so rock 'n roll was the most important component of the phrase "sex, drugs, and rock 'n roll." Next in importance, of course, were drugs. If you didn't use drugs during the 60s, 70s, or early 80s, my guess is you knew someone who did.

The final word, "sex," leads the list in topics that parents have a difficult time talking about to their kids. Throughout the 80s, I worked with kids between the ages of 12 and 18 in residential and psychiatric treatment. Although approximately 85 percent of them had planned to wait until they were older or married to have sex, they in fact had their first sexual experience as teens when they were drunk or high. The odds that drug use will lead to an unwanted sexual encounter are significant. By talking about rock 'n roll, drugs, and sex (in that order) along with some other topics of interest, we can have an open and honest discussion about vital issues and concerns kids have today. Music will be our guide. My hope is to provide practical ideas parents can understand and use.

1

Questions to Think About

Music is a drug of choice for me. It started around 3rd grade. I wanted to become a rock star and on some level, I still do. What stops me is that I have little talent. I played the drums for a while and even joined a band. Needless to say, we never made it out of the garage.

My older sister grew up listening to Motown and what I would consider bubble gum/Top 40 AM radio hits. I would catch her with her friends listening to Lesley Gore's "It's My Party", dancing and singing and pouring their hearts into every word. They would create their own dance to a song by the Supremes or practice kissing the mirror or pillows in order to prepare for what was ahead. (Does anybody remember that?) I would walk in just in time to make a face, act totally disgusted, which is what little brothers are supposed to do, and then leave humming the song I had just heard as I walked back down the stairs, knowing that I wouldn't dare tell my sister (or anyone else for that matter) that I liked her music. Most boys I knew listened to different music than their sisters did back then.

Things are quite different today. I do not come from a religious perspective when talking to parents about music. I attempt to be objective in my approach, which is how I would like to be with you. Please understand that your perception of a particular problem drives your strategy, which is why I want to give you the opportunity to think about the following questions:

- Did you grow up in a home where music could be heard: some of the time, much of the time, or not at all? What type of music was it?

- Were you allowed to listen to any music you wanted, or were there restrictions?

- What type of music did you listen to while growing up? List some of the artists.

- What about these particular artists drew you to their music? The lyrics, the beat, or both?

- Were your parent(s) aware of the music you listened to? Did they approve?

- Has your taste in music changed over the years?

- Has your taste in music changed since you became a parent? If so, in what ways?

- What do you think of the music being created today?

- Has music changed since you were growing up? If so, how?

- Are lyrics in today's music different from when you were growing up? If so, how?

- Do you approve or disapprove of the changes and, if so, why?

- Do you believe music lyrics should be censored?

If you feel comfortable, let your kids know you're reading this book, and discuss your responses with them. Ask them to answer some of the same questions from their perspective. Later, I will share some comments kids and other parents have made.

2

Relating to Music

There was a time when I could name dozens of bands and their members, and quote lyrics that were meaningful to me, and I'm sure many of you could do the same. Why is it that some adults, when music played such an important role in their adolescence, no longer listen to new music or any music at all?

Some of us just grew up. That teenage angst that was once upon us is gone. The music seemed to be able to guide us through life, one day at a time, and it often felt as if our very souls depended on a new album coming out. The music, we believed, would validate our feelings about ourselves and about the world around us.

Parents always ask me, "*How can these kids understand the lyrics? I can't understand a word they are saying. I just cannot relate to these bands!*" Remember, it's not your job to relate to music kids listen to today. These bands aren't playing for you.

Somewhere in the mid-80s, when I was working in a residential treatment center, I was introduced to a much darker form of music, taking place underground and not considered mainstream or alternative. To educate myself in this type of music, I went to the experts: the kids themselves. Their music talked about death, a world filled with doom and a lack of hope, where religion was considered weakness, and lust and evil considered strengths. The music's messages were in direct conflict with most adult moral and religious convictions, which helped set the stage for ongoing power struggles between teenagers and parents. Parents considered this type of music amoral and destructive, while the kids considered it empowering and uplifting, the source of a certain sense of control. Many of these kids formed imaginary relationships with the artists who sang the songs or with the songs themselves. Because most of the kids coming into treatment listened to the same type of music, I became interested in finding out if there was a connection between their drug use and the music they listened to.

Rock 'n roll has always been, and will continue to be, anti-adult, anti-authority, and anti-establishment. It thrives on shock value and addresses issues that many families will not talk about in their own homes. With Wendy Goone, I did a study of music and its potential relationship to drug use in 1986, before rap and hip-hop came to the forefront. Here are some of our findings:

- An individual is likely to be influenced by the music favored by his or her peers (from one-on-one interviews of random groups of teens and a self-report inventory).

- Addicted adolescents and addicted adults prefer heavy metal and rock music (from a self-report inventory administered to adolescents and adults anonymously while in treatment.)

- Music is powerful and can be abused by listeners.

- There is, however, no empirical evidence that music causes addiction.

My assumption is that most of these findings would still hold true today. (With the popularity of rap and hip-hop, the second finding would be different). I've read hundreds of studies that continue to look for a correlation between aggressive types of music and violent, aggressive, or addictive behavior among teens. Will listening to violent lyrics or dark music cause a child to commit an act of violence? If so, was it the music that caused it or was something else going on with that child long before the song was played? Did listening to 60s music make you smoke a joint? Did listening to music that encouraged sexual behavior make you want to have sex? We spend a lot of time, money and energy looking for cause and effect.

I have a better idea: How about some common sense? If you were to put a pair of headphones on and play messages that represented hopelessness, fear, irrational thinking, violent images, and overall exhaustion on a daily basis, how much love and hope would you have in yourself, your neighbor, and society at large? It would make sense to think that negative and pessimistic information—or exposure to violent sounds and sights on a constant and consistent basis—would put most of us on a downward spiral without much hope of returning. However, sometimes what makes sense to adults does not make sense to adolescents. Sometimes that same music that adults find negative and pessimistic some adolescents may find uplifting, provocative, and validating.

George's Story

One thousand young people could attend a concert on any given night and all but one would return home just fine. If you have a child who is going through a difficult time for a variety of reasons, understand that music and other media will have a much greater impact on him or her. I remember a young person, George, who had attempted suicide three times and ended up in seclusion under supervision. I went to talk with him about his suicide attempt and his feelings about being hospitalized. As I sat next to him, he began to cry and shared with me how much he felt like he had become a failure. His comment was, *"I can't even be a success at killing myself. I feel comfortably numb."*

"'Comfortably Numb,' wasn't that written by Pink Floyd?" I asked. We then began a long conversation about Pink Floyd—how Pink Floyd understood him, how he related to their music, and how his parents hated his music and his friends. He admitted that, to him, Pink Floyd's music represented depression, despair, a sense of emptiness, and loneliness. In validating the way he looked at life and the way he felt about himself, Pink Floyd had become his only friend.

I could tell dozens of stories about kids like George who don't have that sense of belonging, who don't only listen to their music, but become enmeshed in it—its culture, values, and norms. They begin to see the music as truth, and they embrace the lifestyle it espouses.

If we as parents are not meeting our kids' needs or helping them meet them in positive ways, they will get their needs met through someone or something else. Most kids understand the difference between reality and fantasy, but we need to be able to recognize when our kids are no longer just listening to their music but becoming enmeshed in its images and themes. Moreover, we need to become more involved in what are children are listening to. Let's start our conversation at the beginning, building the foundation. To build a strong foundation, I encourage families to start with a code of ethics.

3

Code of Ethics

Developing a code of ethics is a strategy I started to incorporate into my workshops with parents and educators during the early- to mid-90s. I received a call from a teacher, after I had encouraged a group of 5th grade students to talk with their parents about creating a code of ethics for their families. This teacher went a step further and made writing the code of ethics into an assignment. She called me to say that parents had contacted her, some upset by the assignment, feeling that the code of ethics was not an appropriate activity to do in school. One family, however, called to praise the assignment, saying that it was the best family time they had spent in years. It took them a half a day to complete the task. Here are some highlights from this family's code of ethics. The code was organized in three sections: *beliefs*, *ideals*, and *rules*. In the *beliefs* section were those things in which they as a family believed as a whole:

- Families should be trusting, honest, and close to one another.

- The way that we treat other people will help make us feel good about ourselves.

- It is important to do our part in society.

- It is important to help those in need.

- It is important to remember people throughout the year, not just at the holidays.

- We must be responsible for ourselves.

- It is only human to make mistakes, but we should learn from our mistakes so that we don't do them again.

- It is wrong to judge another person by the things they have or do not have. People should be evaluated by their hearts and by the way they treat others, not by material possessions.

- We believe that friends should be chosen carefully. We don't believe in hanging around with people who do things we believe to be wrong, such as stealing or doing drugs. Although we don't judge people by what they have or don't have, we do judge people by the things they do and the way they treat others.

The second section is made up of ideals. For most families (including this one), faith, religion, or spiritual beliefs would be listed here.

The last section is the place where each family member agrees to the rules he or she will abide by. For this section, as well as the other two sections, each family member thought about what they wanted to say before meeting as a family. Here is what the 5th grader wrote:

- If anyone ever hurts me or makes me feel uncomfortable in any way, I will tell an adult I trust (the child goes on to list those adults).

- I am responsible for my actions and myself.

- I will tell the truth so I can be trusted.

- I will do my best in school.

- I will live by our family's beliefs and ideals.

- I will do my household chores to contribute to my family.

- I will respect my elders.

Here is what the parents put down:

- We will respect you as a person.

- We will admit when we are wrong.

- We will apologize when necessary.

- We will treat you fairly.

- We will not embarrass you or insult you.

- We will **always** make time for you and be there for you.

- We will always listen to what you have to say.

- We will always believe you, unless you give us reasons not to.

This example of a code of ethics works for this particular family. As with any idea or strategy, it may not work for yours. You can create a code of ethics at any time, but a good time to do so is when your children are in elementary school (between 3rd and 5th grade is ideal)—so there is a solid foundation in place before they start junior high or middle school. As your children develop, so might the code of ethics, but the essence should remain the same. The code of ethics should be signed by each family member and dated.

When I talk to parents about the challenges they face and the feelings they have about what their child listens to or wants to listen to, how they dress, or the posters they decide to decorate their room with, I remind them that the code of ethics can become a foundation. It can give parents a way to respond by saying, "*It's not that what you listen to is trash,*" even if you believe it is, "*but the lyrics are offensive and are in conflict with our code of ethics.*"

4

Listening to the Message

I remember years ago hearing a story about a police officer in California, whose son was going to hear the band Body Count. His son was preparing for the concert by listening to one of their songs called "Cop Killer," when his father walked in and quietly sat on the bed, listening to the song. While the audience would be singing along to the lyrics, his father—the police officer—would be at the concert providing security. His father personalized the song for his son and let him know that the group wasn't just singing about any cop; they were singing about his dad.

I received a phone call from a mom who found some CDs with inappropriate lyrics in her son's room. She had never heard of the artist and was appalled at the content and language the artist used in his music. I have received hundreds of calls from parents just like this one, surprised that their children could be listening to such offensive material. This mother was ready to throw out all of his music, but she knew that would create a massive power struggle, so we came up with a plan. The plan included a code of ethics and a rewriting of one particular song that talked about taking advantage of women and sexual assault. I asked her to talk with her son, using some of the questions included in Chapter 1. She began to ask him about music and particular artists he was drawn to. The goal was to put him in the role of the expert—not only do kids like this, but it also can be a powerful experience when the parent is the learner and the child is the teacher.

It was time for the mother to do the rewriting exercise, but this time I added a twist. I asked the mother to rewrite the lyrics and insert her name in places where the song degraded women. I asked her to send it through the mail, addressed to her son, (the mail can be a powerful tool in many situations) with a note attached asking him to simply read the letter with an open mind and take a day or two before reacting. Needless to say, the son was surprised to read the lyrics and see his mother's name. He told her that the song wasn't about her, that it was addressing other women, women who may have deserved the label due to their behaviors. She pointed out that whomever they were singing about was someone's daughter, sister, or wife, and out of respect to her, asked him not to have that material in their home. It was a conversation that ended in compromise—the son agreed to not have it in the house, but would not promise to stop listening to the band outside of the home or in his car. This satisfied the mom, but more importantly, it opened the door for the possibility of more open conversations with her son.

CD-Swap and CD-Buy-Back

This is a great exercise in exposing your child to different types of music. Take that CD from your child (you know the one, the one you love to hate), and really listen to it. Make some notes and prepare some comments. While you're doing this, give your child or teen one of your CDs to listen to and ask them to do the same thing. This was easier to do 30 years ago, because most kids listened to different music than their parent did. Today, many parents listen to the same music their kids do, so you may have to pull in a relative or friend for this exercise. Sometimes kids may be exposed to other genres of music they never would have been exposed to by doing this exercise.

Another exercise is the CD-Buy-Back. If your child purchases a CD you don't approve of, simply buy it back.

5

Understanding Today's Music

It is important to be aware of what your child is exposed to. Resources abound when it comes to finding out about a particular band or artist. You can now enter almost any band name in any search engine on the Web, and find their bio and lyrics to their songs. Walk into any book or grocery store, and you will find recent magazines that cover different genres. Many of the popular artists will grace the covers of these magazines. For those who have cable, there are many music channels to choose from to help you stay current. Parents always ask me to give them a list of bands or artists they should not allow their kids to listen to. While I can't do that, what I do offer them is an understanding of what a particular artist may be saying in their music, and let them decide if the message is appropriate for their children to hear. Only the artists themselves know what they mean by a word or phrase. Look at the following stanza and write the first thought that comes to mind. What kind of message is this sending to kids?

> *"I hate teachers, I hate school, I hate English,*
> *I hate math, I hate me, I hate you,*
> *I hate people telling me what to do!*
> *Teachers are good for nothing, education stinks!*
> *Classes are for losers, school is for the weak!"*

Do you think this message validates what many kids think and feel about school and their teachers? Did you feel this way? Would you want to hear this on the radio and have it become the new anthem for kids today? Would you want your eight-year-old to listen to this? Let me show you the poem in its entirety:

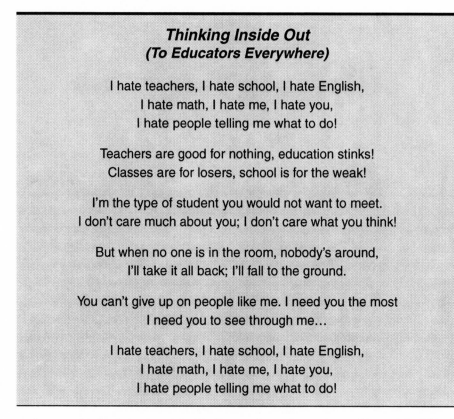

Thinking Inside Out
(To Educators Everywhere)

I hate teachers, I hate school, I hate English,
I hate math, I hate me, I hate you,
I hate people telling me what to do!

Teachers are good for nothing, education stinks!
Classes are for losers, school is for the weak!

I'm the type of student you would not want to meet.
I don't care much about you; I don't care what you think!

But when no one is in the room, nobody's around,
I'll take it all back; I'll fall to the ground.

You can't give up on people like me. I need you the most
I need you to see through me...

I hate teachers, I hate school, I hate English,
I hate math, I hate me, I hate you,
I hate people telling me what to do!

I wrote this back in the early 90s for teachers who were working with difficult students. I wanted them to understand that the kids who disliked them, were most likely the students who needed them the most. I also wanted to make the point that there are songs that need to be heard in their entirety in order to understand the messages. There also are songs full of gratuitous violence and sexual behavior, and hearing the whole song really wouldn't make much difference. Those types of songs, in my opinion, are written for shock value and to sell records. Right or wrong, the constitution protects their right as much as it protects mine to print the poem above and the book you are reading. What matters most is getting information to adults so they can make informed decisions regarding whether certain music and lyrics are appropriate for their children.

6

Enhancing Your Media Literacy

The skill of media literacy helps kids look at television, advertising, print, and music in an educated and constructive way. It involves taking an ad and having the kids talk about what the ad is *actually* selling—popularity, maturity, sex, good times, etc.—compared to what it *pretends* to be selling. Look through several magazines, and look at the ads that are selling alcohol and tobacco. How are these ads being presented to you as an adult? Do they have a picture of an adult or adolescent throwing up in the toilet after a night of partying? Do they show a picture of a baby with fetal alcohol syndrome going through withdrawal? Do they show a picture of a smoker with his five-year-old taking his albuterol treatment? Would these ads make you laugh? Would they make you feel mature or sexy? Do you think these products would sell with that kind of marketing campaign?

Do you think alcohol or tobacco would be illegal today if both products were being introduced for the first time? If an alien being came down to earth and looked at our advertising in regards to alcohol and tobacco, they would interpret those ads to be cool and engaging, sexy and tempting. Yet they would wonder why products that look like they are so much fun to use would include warning signs about the health risks and the possibility that the use of this particular product can lead to death.

I am not saying that these companies do not have a right to market themselves to the consumer. These are businesses that have the right to compete for your dollars like any other business. But don't think for one minute that these companies are not speaking to your kids through their ads, billboards, and other media in hopes of attracting them to their products. You need to understand how your children are being manipulated—beginning at a very young age—into thinking that maturity, sexuality, good times, and developing friendships are connected somehow to drinking alcohol or smoking a cigarette.

Companies spend millions of dollars each year targeting kids as young as three years old, in hopes of convincing them to try their products. See for yourself.

Spend a Saturday morning watching cartoons with your kids and write down every commercial you see for fast food, soft drinks, juices that have little juice in them, cereals, and snacks. Watch for commercials that advertise give-away products that connect fast food with comic book characters or new movies. Think about how fast food companies try to entice your five-year-old into wanting that give-away toy, but the only way you can get it is by pulling into a fast food restaurant. Once again, I am not saying that these companies do not have a right to advertise and market. Advertising has a significant impact on all of us, yet we spend very little time educating our kids in the area of media literacy. I love sweets, high carbohydrate foods, and snacks but, because there is diabetes in my family, I try to limit my intake, and yes, it is difficult. When my first son was born, I told myself that I was going to restrict him from eating sweets. As he turned one year old, we made him a sugar-free cake and presented it to him in front of family and friends. To say that there was not a lot of support in the room would be an understatement. When he turned two, we decided to let him have a sweet every other day. Some of my neighbors supported me in this endeavor, but most did not and would give him cookies, candy, ice cream, and cake without me knowing, believing he was missing out on some two-year-old rite of passage.

Most of my neighbors and family thought I was nuts to think I could limit his sugar intake and thought somehow my son was missing out of the finer things in life. It would have been easy for my wife and me to cave under pressure, to fall into the trap of doing what was considered more acceptable as opposed to doing what we believe is right. Today, we follow the every-other-sweet-day rule. My neighbors are supportive and will even call to ask if today is a sweet day. My family still makes fun but knows we are committed, and, deep down, understands that we are trying to do what is best. We watch ads together that sell sweets and talk about them. We talk about what moderation means and how certain foods are used in the body, some to help us grow and others that may be harmful to us. I can't be responsible for what other parents decide to feed their kids, but I am responsible for what I offer my own kids. Our kids need to understand what is being advertised sometimes is not what the product really is. I am not naive enough to think that, as my kids get older, they won't fall into the sweets, snacks, and fast-food cycle of nutrition. But for now, they eat what we buy for them. We are planting seeds and building a foundation for healthy living. Will it work? Your guess is as good as mine, but remember, it's an odds game. The stronger the foundation, the greater the odds are of raising healthy, drug-free kids.

Here is a list of some of the external sources we are responsible for:

- Print

- Movies (big screen)

- Television (remote control)

- MTV and VH1

- Music

- Cable (satellite dish)

- Cable news

- Talk shows

- Radio talk shows

- Radio

- News shows (local)

- Comics

- Pornography

- Advertising (commercials)

- Packaging (store bought items)

- Billboards

- VCR (rental movies)

- Walkman

- Boom box

- Video camera

- Video games

- Video arcade

- E-Mail

- Cell phone (text messages)

- Computers—chat rooms and Internet surfing

- Computer games

As a parent, I know I am responsible for these external sources, but I realize that there are also places I cannot always be, or times I can't be prepared for. I was watching television with my son, who was four at the time, during an early Saturday afternoon and I went into the kitchen to get something to eat. When I came back in, there was a look of fear on my son's face, as if something came through the television screen and was trying to pull him in. An ad for an upcoming PG-13 movie appeared on the screen during his cartoon show. He just looked at me and said that he was scared. I was livid—this was not the time to be advertising for a PG-13 movie. I immediately called the station to let them know my feelings, but I reached an answering machine. My message lasted as long as the machine allowed. The other day I was watching a baseball game that had a four o'clock start time. During the game, several ads came on to promote TV-14 and PG-13 shows and movies, and I know that several thousand young people under the age of 12 were watching that game. As parents, we must be vigilant in getting our opinions across to those people who have the power to make decisions regarding what our kids are exposed to. It's important to not only complain about a problem, but also to take action. Know your radio and TV station addresses and phone numbers. Write editorials to your local papers. Form parent groups to address some of your concerns in your local area, and teach your children to become smart consumers. Remember that there are many things to teach kids about media literacy. But once again, do not rely on the schools to take the lead. That is our job as parents; it is the school's job to support us.

7

Learning Four Types of Music

I've done workshops for thousands of parents, who always ask questions about the different genres of music out there for kids to listen to. The most popular music kids listen to today, besides mainstream music, is rap and hip-hop along with different types of metal, so I'd like to spend more time talking about those particular genres of music. I will also spend some time focusing on Gothic music, since parents have begun to hear more about it through the media. It is important to know a little about popular genres so you have a starting point to carry on a conversation with your child:

1. *Rave.* Raves are considered more a scene than a type of music, but without the music there would be no scene. The typical audience is older high school students, along with college students and adults. Usually, a rave incorporates techno music with heavy beats, lights, illuminating jewelry, big screens, and anything that may enhance sensation. Rave drugs such as Ecstasy, GHB, Special K, and others may be present. There are hundreds of Web sites that talk about these drugs, including www.nida.nih.gov (the National Institute for Drug Abuse) and www.drugfreeamerica.org. Most kids who attend raves will tell you the main reason they attend is to feel connected. For some kids, it is simply an environment in which to get high.

2. *Techno.* Some consider techno "trance music" due to its beat and rhythm. Beats per minute can surpass 160, but usually stay in the range of 130 to 140 beats per minutes. (An aerobic workout at a high intensity level can measure about 135 beats a minute.) Much of the music played at raves falls into this category, although it changes from time to time.

3. *Mainstream.* Mainstream music encompasses many bands and artists from all genres who have become popular enough to be played on mainstream radio, along with the boy bands, divas, and new reality-TV show winners. Many

21

kids who listen to secular music will listen to mainstream along with alternative music.

4. *Alternative.* Radio stations that call themselves *alternative* really are mainstream. The true alternative radio stations are those on college campuses playing music that most people, except for college students, have never heard of.

Developmentally speaking, most kids from kindergarten through 3rd grade listen to anything their parents put on, or they hear music in a movie or on some of the new reality talent shows. Fourth and 5th graders are little bit more discriminating, and some of these kids can begin to name the artists they like along with the song and its lyrics. Developmentally, 6th graders are very much like 5th graders. During the summer after 7th grade through 8th grade is the time when kids' musical tastes begin to really take shape and solidify. Again, much of this is determined by the foundation you as parents set, along with influences of the peer group.

(For more information on genres, go to www.wikipedia.org. when you enter the website, click on the language you want and then go to search and type in the words, *music genre*. You will then be able to search any genre you like from metal to rap).

8

Rapping About Violence, Gangs and Family Ties

Hip-hop and rap have become very controversial genres of music. Some of this controversy is due to the music's sexual content, but much of the debate lies in and around gangsta rap music, due to its depiction of inner city life and its raw brutality in how it looks at life in general. I remember talking to a group of parents several years ago about the school shootings taking place around the country, when a parent raised her hand and asked this question: *"These school shootings are a terrible thing, but why is it we are just now beginning to pay attention to them?"* Before I could respond to her question, the question had turned into a heated conversation. School violence had received national media coverage, but when the Columbine shootings happened, the country was in disbelief. How could this happen, especially in a white middle class community? Several parents asked if I thought the nation would have paid as much attention to the school shootings if they were happening in low-income neighborhoods. They asked why the country had not taken a more active role in helping and supporting those neighborhoods and communities that experience violence on a regular basis. Everybody cares now, so what took so long? Could that same statement be made about rap music?

Rap came on the scene, along with punk music, around 1976–1977. Music was somewhat indistinct at the time, with stadium rock and disco dominating the airwaves. As summer turned to fall and the temperatures began to drop, so went the music industry as young people all over the country began to look for something new to listen to. Punk exploded onto the scene with bands like the Buzzcocks, the Jam, and the Sex Pistols and—like the Kinks and the Who before them—they brought a much-needed breath of fresh air into the rock industry.

But something else was blowing in the wind. Grandmaster Flash and the Furious Five along with the Sugarhill Gang began to offer kids an alternative to the music scene. Rap music was born, but was not really introduced to the mainstream audience until the Aerosmith and Run-DMC music video "Walk This Way." Groups like NWA and Public Enemy began singing about themes most people would not talk about in their own homes. Several of the *Nu* metal bands today who fuse rap and metal were influenced by Public Enemy and NWA. When do you think mainstream audiences began to pay attention to the messages being presented in rap music?

It goes back to the conversation I had with the group of parents who wanted to know why "*everybody cares now, and what took them so long*". Do you believe most parents are concerned about the messages in some rap music because it's crossed over into the mainstream and is now being listened to by kids all over this country? Would the larger community care about rap music and some of its messages if rap never crossed over into the mainstream? Do you think the same thing happened with Elvis Presley, who introduced music to the white community that was being played predominantly by black rhythm-and-blues artists from years ago? Was the uproar about how he looked, sang, and shook, or was the uproar about introducing white teenagers to blues music in a country that was divided along racial lines?

All of these conversations happened because one person asked the question, "*These school shootings are a terrible thing, but why is it we are just now beginning to pay attention to them?*" It is important to ask these questions if we are to understand the influence music has.

I have talked with thousands of 10-year-old kids who emulate their favorite rap stars through the clothes they choose, language they adopt, and jewelry they wear. Many school administrators have called me with concerns that kids are flashing gang signs, and when the kids are questioned about the signs, they say they saw them in a music video. I remember speaking to a large group of 5th grade students who were having a difficult time getting along with one another, due to their rival taste in rappers. They decided to form small clubs and give themselves names, and then began to flash gang signs, which alarmed the administrators. After introducing myself, I asked the group why they believe kids join gangs. Here are their responses:

- Secret handshake

- Gang signs

- Love

- Friends

- Protection

- Cool colors

- Same language spoken

- Structure

- Discipline

- Fun

- Curiosity

- Respect/self worth

- Drugs/sex

- Money

- I am someone

- I belong

- Excitement

- Weapons

- Identity

- Style of dress (image)

- They always have a leader (role model)

- Act cool

- Home stinks (unhealthy family situation)

- I am not getting any attention

- Lack of role models

- Survival

What thoughts come to your mind after reading this list? I wanted to probe a little bit further, so I asked the kids to form into groups reread the list and come up with the three or four most important reasons kids join gangs. I also wanted them to think about the connection, if any, the music they listened to has with gang activity or gang life in general. Here are the conclusions that we came up with as a group. I want to remind you that these were ten-year-old children who helped develop this list and came to their own conclusions as to why kids join gangs:

- *Survival.* There are children who live in communities where simply walking out the door becomes a game of survival. They feel that many of the rappers talk about this game in their music, and that some rappers provide a sense of hope that if they could make it out and become successful, so could these kids. Some kids are born into families where cousins, uncles, moms, or dads are in a gang, so it becomes a tradition passed from one generation to another. Many kids admitted that sometimes rappers glorify violence and make what happens in a gang sound fun. Most of the kids admitted that their parents didn't like the music due to its violent nature and graphic depictions of inner city life.

- *A sense of belonging.* One of the main reasons kids began to form these clubs was that they want to have a sense of belonging. They want to be part of something bigger than themselves, and they want to feel connected. They want to know that if they were in trouble, picked on, or just needed someone to talk to, they could depend on the group to be there for them. They said that the music provides them with that connection. Some rappers talk about the gang as a family, while others say it is a family until you get in trouble, then they forget about you. The idea of having this group of people for back up and support is an overwhelming motivator.

- *Fun and curiosity.* The music creates a sense of romanticism to some of the kids, as they talk about how cool it would be to be out there on the streets, even if it was just for a little while. One student, who really had experienced the streets, stood up and shared personal stories, as the rest of the kids sitting silently began to understand that maybe, just maybe, it wasn't all that cool after all.

- *Family.* When the kids took a hard look at the list they came up with, it became clear that what so many of them were looking for was a sense of family. I asked them to pull from the list some qualities of a family. They began to compare what a gang offers as opposed to what a family has to offer:

  - Secret handshake

- Gang signs—kind of like a family secret code
- **Love**
- Friends
- **Protection**
- Cool colors
- Same language spoken
- **Structure**
- **Discipline**
- **Fun**
- Curiosity
- **Respect/self worth**
- **Drugs/sex—someone to teach about these things**
- Money
- **I am someone—someone to say nice things about me**
- **I belong**
- Excitement
- **They always have a leader (role model)**

The comments in bold are those that almost all of the kids agreed on are the qualities gang members are seeking. All of us have a responsibility to provide those things to our kids.

There are no easy answers when it comes to addressing gang activity in our communities. We can compete with them by offering service learning, parks and recreation, Boys & Girls Clubs, and several other activities that give our children somewhere to go and something to do. But prevention must begin in the home. Before parents can talk to their kids about gang activity, they need to educate themselves on the topic. If you were to type in the words *gangs* or *gang activity* in any search engine, you would find hundreds of sites that present information about this topic. Most of these sites will give you information on gang attire, language, history of gangs, and type of gangs that may exist in your community. Law enforcement, PTA, and other agencies also offer workshops and training in the area of identifying gang activity.

To find out if your child may be in a gang or thinking about joining a gang, you must first know your surroundings and your local school climate. Call your local police department and school administrators to find out if there has been any gang activity in the last three months. Ask for the name of the gang or gangs that your local school or police department has identified in your area. Like drug use and bullying behavior, denial that the problem may exist in your area (and that your child may be involved) is often the barrier that hinders prevention and intervention strategies from taking place. It is not enough to have safe schools. We need safe communities, and even more importantly, we need safe homes. I know that community mobilization (gathering people from different sectors of the community to take on issues that are impacting and challenging the community) can be time consuming and difficult to do, but the schools cannot solely be responsible for prevention strategies. There is no place for complacency when it comes to suicide prevention, abuse, safety, violence prevention, and drug prevention—only vigilance. I feel strongly that the school's role is to support the parent's role in raising healthy drug-free kids. There are community task forces all over this country working to decrease gang activity in their communities. To take that very first step, parents must sit down and have that conversation with their kids about gangs. It begins with you.

Before we leave this genre of music, parents also need to understand that several rappers and hip-hop groups send messages of hope, faith, and strength to their listeners. I remember years ago listening to the song "Mr. Wendell" by Arrested Development that says *"be strong, serve God only, and know that if you do, beautiful heaven awaits."* The song talks about lessons learned from a homeless person.

Many adults will turn off hip-hop and rap because they don't understand the words, or they believe all rap music to be negative. I remember several parents who were sharing lyrics with me after a workshop one evening. They felt the lyrics should be censored due to their graphic nature. One particular song had gratuitous violence, gunshots as sound effects, and police sirens, all of which can be found in many rap songs. I asked them what the names of the last three videos that they rented for their kids were, all of whom were 7th through 10th graders. Silence. Please understand that all of us must be consistent in the messages we are attempting to send our children. It is a mixed message if we allow our children to see violent PG-13 or R-rated movies and play violent video games, but become upset when we find out they're listening to rap. The genre is not the issue. It is the lyrics that some rappers and hip-hop artists choose to present to its listeners that we need to talk about.

I strongly believe that almost any problem that exists in a school or community cannot be solved without the support and opinions of a cross-section of youth. When adults and young people are equally passionate about changing social norms, and each group is given the opportunity to express their passion in proactive positive ways, magic happens.

(Check out *The Story of Rap Music by* K.Maurice Jones and *The Vibe History of Hip-Hop,* Edited by Alan Light).

9

Going to the Darkest Places: Metal

There are several different sub genres of metal, including: Speed (Helloween), Doom (Candlemass), progressive Black metal (Opeth), Black metal (Emperor) and death metal (Napalm Death). The metal that was coined "satanic," during the early 70s through the late-80s, put parents in an uproar due to its lyrics and messages. I remember reading an article written in *Rock Power* magazine some years ago that predicted rock music was heading in this direction. Here are the stages the author suggested:

Stages of Music

Stage One: 1955–1960—Music pushes sex through sounds and lyrics.

Stage Two: 1965–1970—Music arouses the spirit of young people through drugs, rebellion, and anti-establishment attitudes.

Stage Three: 1970–1980—The quality of the music is unimportant, so it has an addictive sound with loud and violent tones.

Stage Four: 1980s—Rock performers pronounce themselves as messiahs making intimate acquaintances and covenants with Satan.

—Source: *Rock Power* Magazine

It should be no surprise to parents that this type of music would become popular for kids to listen to. What was playing at the movies during the mid-60s and mid-70s? How about *Rosemary's Baby*, *The Exorcist*, and *The Omen*? What was selling in the bookstores? The satanic bible, books on magic, and books on witchcraft. Do you remember what was in the news during this time? What about TV sitcoms? Any games on predicting the future that you can think of that became popular between 1965 and 1976? What about role playing games? Once again, adults went to see those movies, bought those books, and supported the industry, so kids naturally became interested in the genre. Rumors began surfacing that bands like the Rolling Stones and Led Zeppelin, among others, were worshipping the devil as religious leaders began to declare war on evil. But it was Black Sabbath that offered the kids of the very early 70s a very different type of music: an alternative to the peace and love scene that took parents by storm. Back in the early 70s, the band Black Sabbath was on most parents' and religious leaders' hit lists; it was a band misunderstood by most adults who felt it was dark and satanic but understood by the kids who listened to it. Their lyrics ran the gamut of drug use, rebellion, and teenage angst. Adults felt that the band's songs (along with its image) questioned government and faith and glamorized evil. Their first album cover got them enough attention to send them into orbit. Any band—whether it is Black Sabbath, 2 Live Crew, Marilyn Manson, Insane Clown Posse (ICP), or Korn—that gets enough publicity from the adult community will skyrocket into superstardom. How long they stay there depends on how talented the band is to begin with. Black Sabbath is as popular today as they were 30 years ago. By today's standards, Black Sabbath appears tame when compared to the bands that advocate evil over religious values, violence for violence's sake, and explicit sexual content. Musicians today who fit into the darker genres are much more explicit in how they express themselves to their listeners than they were years ago, but so are the movies that we watch and the crime books that we read. The horror genre has changed tremendously in the last 30 years. In the past, Alfred Hitchcock could scare most of us without showing limbs being severed or blood being splattered, but today it is a gore fest. Why should the darkest part of the metal genre be any different? Black Sabbath, if introduced to the adult world today, would not freak out too many parents, but there are bands that would. I had the opportunity to talk to hundreds of kids who listened to bands that represent the darkest part of the genre. I asked them what it was about the music they liked and here is what they had to say:

- *"It explores the dark side. Don't you think we all have a dark side?"*

- *"My family is very religious; this music questions everything I have ever been taught about faith. It talks about things I can't talk to my parents about. It lives out some of my fantasies for me."*

- *"The music; the complexity of the music."*

- *"People look at me weird because of how I dress all black and stuff. They see me coming and move out of the way. I like that."*

- *"I would never go out and do what the music is saying. That is BS. You have to be messed in the head to do what the music is saying. It's not the band's fault. I like the noise behind the messages. The world sucks. Look at all the fighting, and the BS that goes on. The world is full of hypocrites. All these adults who claim to be so religious and then turn around and they treat each other like s**t. This music tells the truth and adults just don't want to hear it. You can worship who ever you want to, but don't tell me who I can worship."*

- *"It is not really about devil worship as much as it is about not believing in anything."*

- *"Some of the bands who play progressive metal really talk more about horror than death and destruction. By horror I mean ghosts and such. It is really complicated music to understand."*

- *"I like listening to doom metal because the lyrics are all depressing. I like the down beats and the way the song moves, slow and powerful."*

- *"I listen to black metal for the music not the lyrics. I can't understand a word they are saying."*

Like rap, all metal sounds alike to most adults, but the messages in most of this music differ from band to band. Where one band's message is anti-faith, another band's message may be to keep on fighting and never give up. There are several Web sites devoted to lyrics from the metal genre that will give you some insight into a particular song (such as www.darklyrics.com).

The darkest part of the genre (Black Metal) is not played on mainstream radio. Most kids and adults have no interest in the messages this music represents. It is an acquired taste. Do most kids who listen to this type of music represent a population of adolescents who are alienated, depressed, or have other kinds of issues in their life? Some adults and professionals in the field would say "yes." It is interesting to me that most teens who get into the darkest part of any genre seem to pay a lot of attention to the lifestyle of the artist, what the music is saying and how that music relates to their lives. That is true for most of us; we listen to music not just for the beat or the sounds that the song creates, but for the message the artist is trying to convey. Do you believe that is a true statement? If your son or daughter listens to metal or gangsta rap that has controversial lyrics or anti faith messages, do they hear those messages, or is it the music that attracts them to a particular song? I wonder what they would say and would you believe their answer? What was important to you at the age of 14 or 16 years old? Was it the beat, the mood the music set, the artist themselves or the lyrics?

I worked with several kids during the 80s who were into the darkest part of the genre. Teenagers who were listening to satanic music came into treatment bringing their satanic bibles with them. Many of these kids shared experiences that were horrifying, and it was difficult for them to understand what was real and what was drug-induced. I remember one incident where several kids came to me frightened and concerned for their safety. Apparently one young man was sitting on his bed quoting passages out of the bible and making threats against other kids. I walked in and found him in a trance. I waited for him to open his eyes and asked him what he was doing that was scaring everyone out of their minds. His response was, "*I was quoting song lyrics from a band. Did you know I was evil?*" This was a teenager who was enmeshed in a culture that romanticized death and evil at its core. He was listening to bands I had never heard of, and I felt that if I was going to reach him, I needed to understand what his music was saying. We worked together for about five months, and I learned how the music filled a void in his life. He felt powerless, alone, and out of control, and the music provided him with power and a sense of control. During his stay, he developed a stronger sense of self, and did not feel the need to be controlled by what he was listening to. It was at that point in the mid 80s that I decided to put together a workshop to educate parents on the different genres that exist, and use music as a catalyst for discussing topics that are relevant to kids.

I have friends who no longer listen to music that talk about sex, violence, or drugs. They won't listen to music with profanity in it. They will no longer listen to some of the music they grew up with, at least not in front of their kids. Recently the Hollywood establishment, some of the same adults who probably criticized Black Sabbath's music years ago, just presented Ozzy Osbourne, the lead singer of Black Sabbath, with a star on Hollywood's Walk of Fame. Go figure.

For more information on Heavy Metal check out *Sound of the Beast-The complete Headbanging History of Heavy Metal* by Ian Christe.

10

Stereotyping:
From Nerds to Goths

Since the Columbine school shootings, Gothic music has received a lot of attention. Usually Goth music has darker themes that revolve around vampires, cemeteries, depression, and general internal angst. Many artistic and very creative kids may sometimes venture into the world of Goth. I asked a group of young people who they listened to and what they watched that would represent a Goth scene. Here is what they had to say:

- *"I like the dark make up and I listen to The Cure."*

- *"Bands like Sisters of Mercy and Kate Bush have a certain sound about them."*

- *"Buffy the Vampire Slayer and Angel."*

- *"We are not evil. Just different."*

- *"There are many different levels of Gothic, some kids say they are Gothic but don't wear the clothes or live the lifestyle. Most Goth kids I know are peaceful, but there are those in the scene who get into the much darker side of Goth. I don't hang with those kids."*

- *"Some Goth kids I know do wear black makeup, clothes and jewelry that fit the scene. Some Goth kids do not eat meat and are pretty peaceful. Some will practice different kinds of spirituality, but that does not make them evil. Some kids will try to look Goth but are really into Metal or Emo, which are bands that have come out of the punk scene whose music is really emotional."*

I remember a crisis call that I answered in which the kids who showed up for the support group seemed to represent every clique in the school. There was one student in particular who was incredibly helpful to her peers. She was bright, sensitive and caring. She was dressed differently from her peers, and had several earrings in each ear, eyebrow, and nose. She wore black makeup and had darkened her hair. I mentioned to her that she should become a peer helper or mediator, but she would have to apply for the position and be chosen by her peers. She began to get a sad look about her and shared that most kids found her weird and felt that her peers would never nominate her. She listened to sad and depressing music on one hand, but on the other hand she would listen to female lead singers whose music was about empowering women. She believed in living a Gothic lifestyle, even if it meant being ostracized by her peers.

Many of the Goth kids I have met through the years are more apt to cut on themselves than they are to hurt other people. That is not to say that all Goth kids are cutters; that is a stereotype that is simply not true. To assume it's true is like saying every kid who listens to rap is in a gang or every kid who listens to dark metal worships the devil, obviously both are untrue. (**To learn more about self injury \cutting see appendix G**)

It is easy to judge people based upon looks and put them in a box. I was walking the halls of a high school when I came into contact with a very interesting-looking, 6'5"-tall, white male with a mohawk, a chain wallet, dressed all in leather, carrying school books in his massive hands. I asked several students and adults who he was, and said that I would like to meet him. I immediately thought "druggie," "skinhead," bully, low-performing student or potential dropout, but I finally found out who he was. He taught me a valuable lesson, this young man I never got to meet, and something we all need to remind ourselves of from time to time. I had labeled him without saying a word to him, and I judged him on appearance alone. Intuition and gut feelings are powerful attributes that exist in all of us to help us survive and spot trouble and avoid unhealthy situations. Nine out of 10 times we may be right, but this was not one of those times. The young man was called a "straight edger." (Kids have told me that several bands that play hardcore music are straight edge). Other students see straight edgers as bright, able to get good grades, drug free (most), religious, and vegetarians.

I spend a lot of time talking to kids and parents about judgment and image. Kids need to understand, if they are going to project an image that goes against the norm, adults as well as kids will judge them. Right or wrong, it happens all the time. These kids need to have a strong sense of self to be able to handle the criticism that most likely will come their way.

Sometimes we as parents are more concerned about our own family's image and what it projects to the community at large than we are in allowing our kids to be who they are. Sometimes we label our own kids and judge them unfairly because we want them to be miniature versions of ourselves or of the neighbors' kids down the street. Most of the time we don't do it intentionally or maliciously, but out of love and caring for our kids. As parents, we need to be cautious about labeling and judging our own children, as well as our neighbors' children.

I am often asked by middle school administrators to work with students representing different groups who may have a conflict with one another. I developed a workshop in the early 90s to help kids identify the different cliques that existed in their schools. I asked kids between the ages of 10 and 14 to comment about cliques they have in their schools, listing the groups along with the stereotypes existing within each. I wanted them to think about questions like:

- What kinds of music do these kids listen to?

- How well do they do in school?

- Are they good at sports?

- Are they popular?

- Are they likely to attempt suicide?

- Are they likely to be sexually active?

- Do they do drugs?

- Are they liked by their teachers?

Here are the lists of cliques these kids came up with and the characteristics they identified for each group:

Nerds

- wear high-water pants

- do well in school

- are computer- and math-minded

- do not use drugs

- are not involved in sexual activity

- are not involved in gangs

- are not accepted by mainstream students

- are at risk for attempting suicide

- are often teachers' pets

- are never in trouble

- read often

- button their shirts all the way up

- do not have a lot of friends

Snobs

- are stuck-up

- are rich

- are teachers' pets

- are air-heads

- are annoying

- show off and brag

- are usually white

- are loud and try to get attention

- are spoiled brats

- get good grades

Wiggers/Oreos

- listen to rap

- are concerned with image (pants, hats, clothes in general)

- are white trying to be black or black trying to be white

- are in interracial couples

- do drugs

- have sex

- try to talk street

- get in trouble with the law (sometimes)

Freaks

- do drugs

- are mostly white

- dye hair (funky hair style)

- engage in "five-finger-discount" (stealing)

- listen to heavy metal/death metal

- cause trouble at school

- are not smart/don't try

- do not have a good home life

- have low self esteem

- are easy (girls)

- do not have good morals

- are depressed

- can be suicidal

- sometimes are into Wicca

- can be Satanists

- have body piercing

- wear a chain wallet

- have sex

- get in trouble with the law

- are not liked by teachers

- think that school is a joke

- can be Goth

Posers

- lie about skating

- try to be something they are not

- wear pants that do not fit

- say they listen to The Misfits

- do drugs

- try to get sex

- get poor grades

Preps (see Snobs)

- are vain

- suck up to teachers

- really care what other people think

- dress nicely

- are popular

Skaters

- wear baggy clothes

- have skateboards

- get bad grades

- are not well liked

- listen to aggressive music

- wear combat boots (docs)

- wear long green jackets

- smoke pot

- use inhalants

- are not liked by teachers

Rednecks

- wear tight jeans

- get drunk

- listen to blue grass/country music

- are racist

- go hunting

- get bad grades

Jocks

- are not smart

- are sports minded

- do drugs (but their parents don't think that they do)

- are popular (but many bully other young people)

- are liked by teachers

This information comes from thousands of kids between 10 and 14 from a variety of schools. Most of the descriptions are stereotypes that some kids and parents perceive to be true. Most students claim no affiliation to any one group.

Did you belong to a certain group when you were in middle or high school? Which group did you belong too? Would your friends have put you in the same group you put yourself in?

One of the most important values we can instill in our children is the ability to judge a person by their behavior and character. The best part of this particular workshop is the conversation that begins to evolve around the stereotypes, because it makes kids take a hard look at themselves and how they treat other people. They realize so much of what they are basing their opinions on has nothing to do with who the person really is.

11

Identifying Signs of Trouble

How do you know when your kids are in trouble? There are genres of music that are not popular with the average kid. One never really knows what attracts a certain adolescent (or adult, for that matter) to a particular type of music. Most kids will listen to whatever their peer group is into, so that's where you have to start. Do you know your teen's peer group? Do you know any of their friends' parents? Do you know how other areas of your child's life are going?

There are genres of music that can be quite dark, quite racist, and quite enticing to those who are looking for a place to belong. Even kids who are stable, well rounded and quite balanced can be taken in by a culture they aren't prepared to handle. A parent's nightmare is to believe they are doing everything right, and still have a child make poor choices. One of the best ways to know if your child is being influenced in a negative way through music they are listening to is to know your child. Here are some guidelines to consider in getting to know your child and evaluating the impact of various influences on his or her life:

- *Check in.* Connect with someone who you trust at your child's school. Check in with them from time to time.

- *Walk the halls.* When I worked treatment, I would go into a nearby middle or high school and just walk the halls to get a feel for the student body—their likes, dislikes, clothes and so on. It is important to have a baseline when trying to figure out if your son or daughter is acting outside the norm. Of course, this rule does not always apply to every issue, as in some communities it is the norm to use drugs or be sexually active.

- *Pay attention.* Any *extreme* mood changes, habits, *value disintegration*, or overall belligerence toward you or other people are red flags that something is going on. It is quite normal for kids to change friends, clothes, hairstyle, and image during different developmental stages of their lives. What becomes more important than the external features that change is that the respect they have for themselves and for those around them stays consistent through the changes. They must be able to withstand the pressure they may receive from others who gravitate towards them due to the image they are projecting. If they do not have a strong sense of self and a solid support system and foundation in place, then the odds of them falling into the path of self-destructive behavior increase considerably.

- *Look for balance.* It is quite normal for kids to question the foundation you believe in. But a child who becomes influenced through music loses all flexibility and balance in his life. Music becomes the way, and all values, opinions, and beliefs take on the personality that the artist is offering its listener.

- *Don't assume there's a problem.* Please understand that music and other media influences are only one area of a child's life. It is an area that becomes a helpful tool in identifying possible problems and challenges a young person may be having in their lives, but it is not always an indicator of trouble. There are people, whether teenagers or adults, who can be caught up in the darkest genres of music and are not in trouble. It may be the energy, the beat, or the overall sound of the music that they like, but they never take ownership of the lyrics. They are able to deflect the negativity and use the music for entertainment value alone. Even with new distractions such as the internet and video games, music is still one of the most powerful forms of communication we have today and it can be abused by listeners.

Many of us as adults can look back and say we have been through the drugs and the music scene and survived. We went through the hair bands and power rock of the 80s with messages that we can take on the world, to the grunge and industrial scene, which appeared to offer less hope and more despair. Some of us went through the disco and cocaine scene or the punk movement, where everything seemed to be about anarchy, politics and revolution. So we expect our kids to do the same without recognizing what has changed.

We have watched hundreds of violent movies, love to read books that have violence in them, have seen thousands upon thousands of television shows that feature acts of violence, and watch hours upon hours of news broadcasts and news channels that continue to feed off our desire of wanting to hear and see stories that pertain to violence. Look at us now. *We turned out okay, didn't we?*

We as adults have a responsibility to set examples for our young people. We rent PG-13 movies for our eight-year-olds and R-rated movies for our 13-year-olds, thinking the violence will look diminished on a 32-inch screen compared to the movie theatre screen, and yet we're appalled at the lyrics they find fascinating.

We seem to be at ease showing violent movies to our kids, but draw the line at showing them movies that may have sexual overtones in them.

Many of the movies, and music of the late 60s and early 70s, were full of anti-authority, anti-government and pro-drug use messages, but some of the music offered a sense of hope and unity. As young people, we believed we could overcome any obstacle with the help of friends and neighbors, and together we could make a better world. Parents need to understand that those same messages still exist in music today. Kids are just as much into their music today as we were yesterday. Parents continue to say to me "*I just don't understand the music of today. It just does not make sense. It's rude and abrasive and I don't want my kids to listen to that garbage.*" That garbage is what kids are listening to today. It is their generation, not yours. You have to decide, as a parent, which music is in conflict with your code of ethics and which isn't. (There is an activity in the back of the book to do with your teen; to help you explore what you listened to while growing up and what your kids are listening to now. There are some risks involved, so make sure you understand the activity before you begin.)

I was at a Teen Institute dance with 200 students and 40 adults several years ago. Teen Institute is a four-day, three-night retreat for teams of four to six students from different schools. These students were potential leaders who were asked to come together to create an action plan for their school and community. During the dance, one couple began to get a little risqué with their dancing. They were doing a dance that a lot of kids were doing at the time. An adult asked me to break up the couple or shut down the dance and I politely said "no." The adult ran to gather other adults to rally on her side, as she felt the kids were inappropriately using their body language to entice one another, possibly into sexual activity, maybe encouraging them to sneak out later that evening.

We are asking our children to not drink or use other drugs. We are asking them to wait until marriage to have sex. We are trying to extend the age of when a teen can begin driving, because we feel it would be in their best interest to do so. We put more academic pressure on them than any other generation has had to bear, and are measuring their ability to succeed solely on standardized test scores. We seem to only hear about the kids who are into unhealthy behavior, not the ones who are trying to help their fellow peers, themselves and their community. They are living in a time where adults seem to be arguing over what used to be absolutes and they are a generation who must now live in a post-September 11th world that appears to be based in fear and uncertainty. We need to use some common sense, and choose our power struggles wisely. In his song, "The Times They Are A Changin'", Bob Dylan talks about how we should not criticize all the things we do not understand. He shows that we have a choice in this new world and new generation of kids, and that the message to adults that was shared 35 years ago is still relevant today. *"Get out of the new one if you can't lend your hand, oh the times they are a changin'."* Yes, we need to have more adults on the same page. Yes, we need more adults talking about solutions as opposed to focusing on the problem and yes...the times are changin', but please, let the kids dance.

12

The Perfect High

Do you have a song that can bring you back to a moment in time, where you can smell the grass after a cool rain, and feel the breeze brush against your brow? A song that can break a mood or create one? A song that brings back friends who you have not seen for years? A song that simply asks you to remember when?

I remember Peter (not his real name), who came to me wanting to know if there was such a thing as a perfect high. He explained that music was a perfect high for him because he was a guitar player, but he needed to be high to really experience the music. I often hear this today from kids who "preload" before they go to a concert, like many adults who grew up in the 60s, 70s, and 80s did. Peter had just entered treatment, and was looking for answers to his very young and out-of-control life. I asked him if he had ever heard the poem by Shel Silverstein called "Baba Fats." "*Baba Fats?*" he responded. "*You know, Baba Fats, the dude who lives high up in Nepal, the guru who can tell you where to find the perfect high. You see, the boy in the poem was looking for that perfect high, just like you, Peter.*" I began to explain to Peter how the young man in the poem became obsessed with finding the perfect high. The young man had to go through hell and back, and even when he reached Baba Fats and was told the truth about the perfect high, the young man threatened him because he didn't want to believe that the perfect high existed within himself. So Baba Fats sent him on his way again, making up a story about how a perfect high really does exist, basically telling the young man what he wanted to hear. And so the poem concludes, "'*Well, that is that,' says Baba Fats, sitting back down on his stone, facing another thousand years of talking to God alone. 'Yes Lord, it's all the same, old men or bright-eyed youth, it's always easier to sell them some s**t than it is to tell them the truth.'*"

Peter's eyes began to swell up, as if to say that he too had been searching for that perfect high, but instead found himself in treatment, alone and scared and not knowing what was going to happen next. I wished Peter had said those things, but instead he asked if he could call his parents and go home. Treatment is hard work, and Peter would rather have done time somewhere else than to have to talk about his problems, his addiction, or his life. I put him on the think chair, a chair that faced the front door, looking outside to freedom. I asked him to think about Baba Fats and become that boy in the story. I told him that if he ran, I would not chase him. Running had become a way of life for him and the weight of his world would continue to drag him down, and I would not become an obstacle for him to jump over in pursuing his perfect high. Peter didn't run that night. He sat for more than an hour in silence, watching and waiting for some sign to magically appear. There was no magic, no sign, just a young man, sad and confused with nowhere to run. Finally we looked at each other and laughed, knowing that the outcome was inevitable, knowing that Peter was tired of running and tired of being sold s**t. There are thousands of high school kids who seem to be searching for the perfect high. My hope is that they will all cross paths with a Baba Fats in their life, before they find themselves sitting in a think chair like Peter.

13

Talking About Drugs

If you want parents to come and listen to a drug talk, don't call it a drug talk. Send a letter telling the parents that the school system is redistricting and they need to attend this very important meeting. Apologize when the auditorium is full, and state that the letter was a mistake and continue on with your drug talk. It just might work.

One time, when speaking to a group of 150 5th graders, I asked them what they were sick and tired of hearing when it came to drug talks. A boy in the back of the room stood up and confidently stated that he knew all about drugs and that his parents felt pot should be legalized. He was tired of speakers coming in and telling the kids not to do drugs and that drugs could kill them. He already knew that. He then proceeded to ask me if I had anything different to say. I had to think fast to reply to such a sophisticated and mature speaker. I replied, "*Yes, I do have something different to say to all of you today. As a matter of fact, I challenge you—all of you. If you do not learn something new today, I will perform for you. I will do anything you want me to do that is legal inside this room.*" I went on to talk about the rules of the challenge and how it was based on them being honest and saying that they did not learn anything new in order for them to take the challenge. The young man sat down as the rest of the audience was eager to now hear what I had to say. That talk took place in 1990, and ever since that time it has become a way for me to begin my workshops with kids. In the field of prevention, you learn quickly that you must engage kids and speak to them on their level. I really believe that if you are going to work with kids as a professional, or try to communicate with your kids as a parent, you have to understand a little bit about what is going on in their culture and world in general. Remember that your perception of a problem drives your strategy. So when the "drug conversation" comes up, or, for that matter, any conversation that relates to teen issues, have the insight to understand why you feel the way you do. To get back in touch with that insight, think about these questions:

- Describe the overall problem of drug use (if any) in:
  - Your local school
  - Your community

- Describe what you know about any of the following substances: (pick one)
  - Alcohol
  - Marijuana

- Should marijuana be legalized? (Please explain.)

- Did you grow up listening to music with pro-drug messages?

- Do you look at addiction as a disease, learned behavior, or a combination?

- Do you view alcohol the same way you look at other drugs?

- Did you grow up in a family where alcoholism was present?

- Do you have a "no-use" message in your home?

- If you did use substances as a teenager, how much information should you give your kids about your past use?

- Do you think there is a relationship between drugs and sex?

- Did you have to drink or use other drugs to enjoy yourself at a party?

- Did a concert sound good to you only if you were drunk or stoned?

- Do you remember your high school or college days? Do those good times revolve around drug use?

Kids today are being sold the same messages in today's music and movies that we were 20 or 30 years ago. The glamorization of drug use and the romance and relationship that kids develop with their drug of choice is just as prevalent today as it was when we were young. Is there anything that can be done to lower the risk of your child getting involved with drugs? Before we can talk about this, let's look at some characteristics of a healthy family.

14

Getting Through the Turbulent Times

I have asked kids and parents alike to identify characteristics that make up a healthy family. Here is what they had to say:

- Honesty

- Open door policy—kids can talk to parents about anything

- Trust each other

- Predictable

- Open communication

- Logical rules and consequences

- Rituals

- Feelings can be expressed

- Respect

- Healthy atmosphere

- Treated as individuals

- Freedom

- Sense of responsibility

- Sense of belonging

- Attempt to receive equal piece of the pie

- Feel safe and secure

- Clear boundaries

- Stability as opposed to disorganization

- Feel loved

- Feel listened to

- Can express anger appropriately

- Sense of spirituality

- Encouraged

- Sheltered sensibly

- Allowed to make mistakes

- Taught to feel responsible *to* others, not *for* others

- Live by a code of ethics

How many of these characteristics do you see in your family today? How many existed in the family you grew up in? There have been volumes of self-help books written on the subject of healthy families. Most of these characteristics come up in all of them. Is it possible to be all of those things all of the time? All families are dysfunctional at one time or another. The difference between a healthy family and an unhealthy family is that the healthy family, when hit with obstacles and roadblocks, works together to overcome and meet those challenges. The unhealthy family stays stuck, repeating the same behaviors while implementing the same strategies, yet expecting different results. There are kids who come from unhealthy families who do just fine. There are also kids who come from healthy families who just make poor choices. The whole idea of prevention is to increase the odds that a child will be given the tools to make it through those turbulent times, regardless of the type of family he or she comes from.

When you were a teenager, did you act out? Did you listen to music or watch movies that were in conflict with your parents' values? Did you drink, smoke pot, or use other drugs? If you answered "yes" to some of these questions, do you know why?

To learn why kids act out, once again I went to the experts—middle and high school students—and asked them why they think kids their age act out. Here is what they said:

Why Kids Act Out

- They are testing limits, want to be different, and want to get their parents' attention.

- Their parents are getting divorced (some of them).

- Their parents are using drugs. Please understand that many parents smoke pot in front of their kids. I remember talking to a young man who was turned on to marijuana by his parents when he was 12 years old. I have worked with several young people who have had similar experiences.

- Abuse may be going on in the home or outside of the home.

- They can't make or find friends for a variety of reasons.

- They are not doing well academically.

- There is a sense of hopelessness, fear and\or frustration.

- They feel a sense of shame and lose all confidence in themselves.

- Their basic needs are not being met.

- They cannot meet parents' expectations.

- They cannot meet own expectations.

- They have safety and security issues.

- They have no sense of belonging.

- They do not understand what is not in their control (parent drug use, divorce, depression).

Weekend Warrior or Addict?

Many of the high school kids cited these as some of the reasons so many of their peers turned to alcohol and other drugs. They asked me why I thought kids used drugs and my response was simple. People do drugs to change the way they feel. I don't care if we are talking about caffeine, wine, beer, hard liquor or pot. If it doesn't change how you feel, most people wouldn't drink it, smoke it, eat it, or inject it. What would be the point? I asked them what their definition of a "weekend warrior" was. Most of them began to laugh and clap out loud. They felt that 70 percent of all the kids they knew were weekend warriors. They are good kids who pull good grades and have average respect for their parents, but party like crazy on the weekends. I began to write on the board what a typical school week might look for these kids:

Monday—Tell war stories: who hooked up, who puked, who acted obnoxious, who made people laugh, and so on.

Tuesday—Go to school and recoup.

Wednesday—Put out your feelers for the next party.

Thursday—Make your plans for the weekend.

Friday—Secure your plans.

Friday night into Saturday—Party.

Sunday—Sleep and get back to normal routine.

I asked the kids how they would know if their friends crossed the line from weekend warrior into an addiction. I also asked them if it was the alcohol and other drug use that became the bond that held their group of friends together, and when—if ever—would they tell an adult that they trusted that some one in their group needed help. I asked them, "*If you are all using together and one of you develops a problem, what does that say about your use? Can any of you in the room put fourteen days together without being under the influence of a drug?*" The laughter and smiles turned to deep thought and the comment "*He can't be talking about us*" was being mumbled under their breath.

One very brave high school student stood up and began to tell her story about being in recovery. She said how difficult it was being in a high school where everybody parties. (Most kids' perception is that everybody parties). She hears the war stories on Monday morning and runs like hell knowing she could be right back into that behavior in a heartbeat. It just wasn't the high that she missed, but the scene. Her old using friends, places they would hang, and the music she would listen to. If she heard a song on the radio from a band she used to get stoned to, she had to turn it off. *"It is amazing how much time went into the planning, thinking about, buying, and consumption of the drug. You guys don't understand how quickly addiction can grab you. It's not like I woke up one day and prayed to God and asked to become an addict! Thanks for listening."* With that, she grabbed her stuff and walked out. What courage this young woman had and how many demons she still had left to fight. After the brief silence, we came up with a list of what kids need from their parents. Here it is:

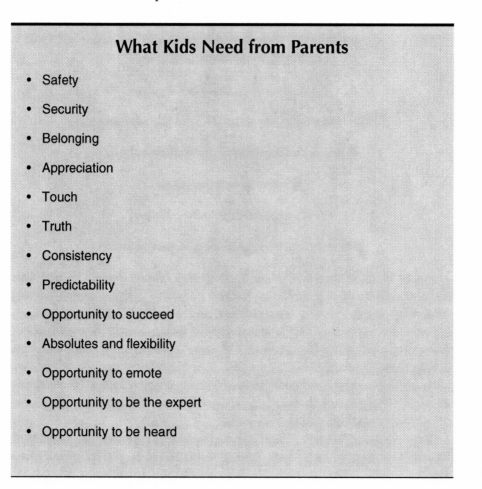

What Kids Need from Parents

- Safety

- Security

- Belonging

- Appreciation

- Touch

- Truth

- Consistency

- Predictability

- Opportunity to succeed

- Absolutes and flexibility

- Opportunity to emote

- Opportunity to be the expert

- Opportunity to be heard

- Time to socialize

- Time to do nothing

- Trust

- Responsibility

- Time

- Love

- Consequences

- Involvement

The bell began to ring and it was time to go. Some of the kids thanked me, for a variety of reasons, and I could tell it was a waste of time for others. Sometimes you just never know what is going to stick, and who you are going to touch. You just have to keep trying.

15

Long Haired Country Boy

I remember rocking in a chair on the porch during the summer of 1978. I was in summer school and the atmosphere around the campus was very relaxed. I can still smell the flowers and see the movement of the leaves on the trees. We had a stereo set up where the speaker could be placed near the window, so everyone else could hear what we were playing. Someone in the house put on a Charlie Daniels song called "Long Haired Country Boy," and as the words started to circulate in the air ("*I get drunk in the morning, I get stoned in the afternoon*"), several people came up on the porch and started to philosophize about life. The song talks about freedom and independence, and about making your own way and not letting anyone else tell you how to live.

That song, along with so many others, became sort of an anthem for a generation searching to find itself. The music written between 1966 and 1976 is filled with drug references that many kids related to independence and freedom. Drug references in music date as far back as the 1930s and 1940s, when much of that music with drug and sexual overtones was banned from any kind of airplay. But it was really the decade between 1966 and 1976 that a generation embraced the messages. Some of the country's highest documented drug use occurred in the late 70s into the early 80s. I read recently that Charlie Daniels will no longer sing the song "Long Haired Country Boy" or, if he does, he will sing it with the "drunk" and "stoned" lyrics omitted. We need to allow artists to grow along with the listener, and give them the opportunity to express themselves at different stages in their lives. We can choose to listen or not. On that summer day long ago, the song "Long Haired Country Boy" did not represent drug use to me; instead, the song represented a sense of independence and belonging. For a brief moment in time, that song brought together a few strangers to talk about life in the hot sun. "*Man that sounded good.*" That sounds exactly like kids today when they are trying to justify the music they listen to. That sounds exactly like many adults who are trying to justify what they listen to versus what their son or daughter is listening to. Plain and simple, "Long Haired Country Boy" is about lying around and getting wasted and not caring about what other people think. That was an expression voiced by hundreds of bands. Like other songs from that era, the artists depicted drug use as a way of self-expression, independence, and freedom. Many of the bands and artists during the late 60s, 70s, and into the 80s were drug users themselves, so it makes sense that so many of the lyrics expressed positive attitudes towards drug use. As the conversation for the legalization of marijuana heated up into the 90s, a new wave of lyrics were being written that expressed pro-marijuana use, with explicit remarks pertaining to just not the use of marijuana, but the glorification of drug use in general.

16

Arguing Pot versus Alcohol

I had a conversation with a group of students about the role music plays in getting drunk or stoned. They shared that it was essential to choose the right music for the mood. One student shared that at parties; a lot of time is spent picking out the night's music. *"It has to fit what we're about,"* they said. We then got into a conversation about why pot should or should not be legalized. I shared with them an experience I had doing a talk show at the Fox Theatre in Atlanta. The talk show featured three of us: a recovering young person, a rock star and me.

I was asked if I would be willing to appear on the television show *Wavelength* (which has since been cancelled) to talk about the legalization of marijuana. I knew it was a setup, and that my role would be to talk about why pot should *not* be legalized with the rock star, who felt strongly that it should be legalized, and with the recovering individual somewhere in the middle. The audience was pro-marijuana. As we began our discussion, the rock star had several facts that he shared with the audience about alcohol use and misuse. These facts were the basis of his argument as to why pot should be legalized. He shared statistics on alcohol-related deaths and went on to say that there were no known recorded overdoses from taking pot. He then went on to state all of the positive ways pot could be used. I thought about what he said and what his motivation was for saying it. When I listen to kids who want marijuana to be legalized, they have the same argument as the rock star. What teens seem to forget is even if pot were legalized, it would not be legal for them to use. I took the next five or six minutes to respond to the rock star's comments. Here are some of the questions and statements I had for him, as well as for high school kids I talk to regarding legalization of marijuana:

- What would be the amount of pot a person could smoke before they got behind the wheel of a car?

- Who would regulate the sale of marijuana?

- If kids get alcohol from their parents or older siblings, what would we do to prevent that from happening with pot?

- Would businesses open their doors and sell pot like we now sell alcohol?

- How would we go about choosing the neighborhoods that would be responsible for growing pot? Would you want your own children living in these neighborhoods?

- Since there are a number of addicts already in our country today, how would legalizing pot help them to acquire some sense of sobriety?

- I may not know a young person who died from a pot overdose, but I do know teens who: dropped out of school; had sex when they did not plan to; disrespected themselves; lost their drive to succeed; and moved on to other drugs when pot got boring, or the high just didn't do anything for them anymore. Don't you think we should reevaluate the question of legalizing pot?

I used this argument several times in the mid 90s while working with high school students, in hopes of combating some of the pro-drug messages kids receive in music today. I still use some of the questions with kids and parents alike, who feel that marijuana is harmless and should be legalized.

Addictive Behavior

Is addictive behavior a character flaw, some weakness within ourselves that we just need to learn how to control? Is it caused by our environment, the family we grew up in, the people we hang around with, the experiences we have, is it learned? Or is it a disease, progressive, with an outcome of emotional, spiritual, and or physical death if not stopped? Is it passed through the genes like some other illnesses and the only way of avoiding the illness is to not drink or use other drugs? At some point during this conversation, all the theory gets thrown out, and there is only one bottom line. If you fall into a large hole, will you spend most of your time beating yourself up because you fell in or will you put your energy into figuring out how to climb out? It doesn't matter how teens become addicted; what matters is how we help them get out of the hole.

17

Creating a Stronger Sense of Self

Where do you believe self esteem comes from? Is it something we are born with? Is self esteem something we learn? Before I share some strategies with you, I would like you to consider these questions:

1. Did you grow up with a strong sense of self?

2. Does the music you listen to now encourage you to take on life's challenges? What about the music in your past?

3. Growing up, did you have adults that modeled a strong sense of self?

4. What do you project to your kids? Are you a self assured individual who is allowed to make mistakes or an individual who has self doubt and a lack of confidence? How do your kids see you?

There have been times in my life when self doubt and lack of confidence seemed to outweigh any positive attributes I may have had. Many of us as young people and now as adults go through various stages of self esteem, riding on a wave of confidence to questioning our desire to move forward. For many, faith, family and friends get us through those difficult times and help us to believe in ourselves, even when we do not. Often, when we were teenagers, music helped us through those difficult times and created in us a determination and strength that we could overcome obstacles and move forward. Music offers kids today that same sense of empowerment and strength. Many teenagers today look to music as a catalyst for beginning that philosophical conversation that they have with themselves, in order to pull them out of what ever hole they sunk themselves in. I get concerned about young people who use sex and drugs to medicate their insecurities and lack of self esteem. I also get concerned about those young people who have an inflated sense of self and who develop a lack of empathy towards others. At times, these young people choose unhealthy behaviors to get involved in. I do believe self esteem is a combination of biological seeds (which we have no control over) and learned behavior that we can model, shape and positively reinforce. Let us continue to focus on those things we have control over as opposed to those we do not.

The following are some points and strategies I share with parents to help their children create a stronger sense of self:

- Remember, kids are like sponges: they soak up anything and everything they can get their hands on. I believe parents do the best job they can with the tools they have to work with, but we need to keep putting tools in our toolbox. We need to be aware of what we are soaking our children with.

- Allow the child to feel good about himself through community service and good deeds. Praise him when the praise is warranted and/or unexpected. "*Pay attention to their good deeds as much or more than you pay attention to their grades.*" (This is from a book by Dennis Prager called *Think a Second Time*.)

- Allow children the opportunity to learn and grow from their mistakes.

- Understand your own temperament and your child's. Are you worriers? Do you make friends easily? Do you transition well? Do you have a low frustration tolerance level? Do you get angry easily? Are you sensitive? Do you have empathy for others? What makes you unique?

- **Try not to** compare siblings to one another.

- Help your children identify their gifts. Many times, I will ask kids to tell me what their gifts are. I ask them to share what they do well and what they have to offer others in the way of character. Many kids have a difficult time with this exercise. It is much easier for them to come up with a list of things they do wrong. I ask them to think of an adult in their life whom they believe has gifts to share and read these gifts to the group. Many kids find it safer to agree with other people's lists than to write their own. Doing a gift list for your own family is a great exercise.

- Evaluate your own expectations that you have for your child. Give him the opportunity to live his life, not complete yours.

- Provide opportunities for success beyond academics.

- Provide your children with a variety of healthy adults other than yourself.

- Teach them problem solving, decision-making, and management skills, i.e. expression of feelings, anger management, and so on.

- **Emotional instability can negatively impact academic performance**.

Many adults feel that self-esteem is overrated. We spend too much time worrying about how kids might feel about a certain situation, so we protect them through unwarranted compliments and praise, and tell them they did a good job when they really didn't. I remember talking to a 14-year-old boy who was showing a picture he drew in class to other classmates and asking for their opinions. They all told him it "sucked" (their words). He laughed about it and agreed with them, and then asked some kids how he could have drawn it differently. Another 14-year-old may have had a very different response to the phrase "it sucks." Much of that depends on how each child hears and internalizes criticism and how much praise and encouragement the child receives as opposed to negative comments and criticism. Kids can see right through false and insincere praise, but support, encouragement and positive feedback can go a long way to enhance your child's self-esteem.

We have this idea today that character education should start in the schools and be reinforced in the home. Do you think that is a good idea? Should schools be responsible for teaching character education? Do you have a character "word of the week" written somewhere in your home? Do you remember the character words written on the report cards in the 50s and 60s? I remember my parents were as interested in my teachers' comments about how I was doing with those character words as they were in my grades. I hear from so many parents about how disrespectful kids are today, and I hear the same thing from teachers. Every school system has rules and policies in place for dealing with disrespectful behavior towards adults and towards other peers. What policies or rules do you have in place for disrespect in your home? I ask you: if we as parents are responsible to teach and model healthy character for our children, then who are the parents that are expecting the schools to teach it? Before we judge our neighbors or the parents down the street for raising kids with poor character, let us all be sure our own homes are in order. There are intrinsic personality traits that kids develop on their own, out of our control, such as drive, ambition and so on. It is our job to do the best we can with providing some sense of balance in their life.

Jill's Story

I got a call several years ago from a mother whose daughter ran away. She was a good student up until two months prior, the mom said. The woman had no insight into what might be happening to her daughter. I began to ask her questions to see if I could make some sense of what was going on. One of the first questions I ask parents when I am trying to find out what may be going on, is to share with me what their room looks like and what music they listen to. Sometimes you get lucky. This was one of those times. The mother walked upstairs and opened the door to her daughter's room to find several pictures of rock bands on her wall. She asked me if I had heard of any of them and I replied, "*Yes to some of them, but give me a couple of hours and I will call you back.*" I went out and purchased some of the CDs I had not heard, and started to piece some things together. This was a teen who was becoming enmeshed into a subculture of drug use, but at the same time feeling validated by some song lyrics—it was all there. I brought the CDs back to the office and called the mom. I began asking her about the possibility of her daughter using drugs, knowing this is every parent's nightmare. I asked her if she had lost any weight and wanted her to look through her closet for certain kinds of clothes and accessories. I told her that there is a possibility that she was taking ecstasy. I asked her if she could locate any poetry or writings that her daughter may have left lying around. (People will send me faxes of poetry and writings that 50 to 60 percent of the time turn out to be song lyrics.) She found some notes that read,

"*Here's to the losers, substance abusers, to the rejects, all the imperfects, I think we're beautiful, no matter what anyone says I think we're beautiful.*" Those are lyrics to a song called "The Losers", by Warrior Soul. The daughter, Jill, ultimately did return home and got help, and I had a chance to talk with her about her recovery a few months later. She did not have many friends except for the band that validated how she was feeling. That song spoke to her. Someone thought she was beautiful, even if that someone was a person she had never met.

Kids with a low sense of self become more vulnerable to the pressures of trying to resist drug use. It becomes simple for them to find a sense of belonging within the drug culture because that culture is very accepting. The same can be true for kids who have a grandiose opinion of themselves because they know for sure that nothing can happen to them. Many people consider addiction a disease of the self. It wraps itself around you and squeezes as it tells you nothing is wrong. It tricks you into thinking you have complete control over the situation and that you can stop any time you want. What happens sometimes is that it is not the low self-esteem that gets in the way, but the narcissistic attitude that the world revolves around the addict and you are in complete control and in a position of power to do something about it.

18

Using Secret Codes

Most kids, until they are seven or eight years old, learn what tobacco and alcohol can do to the body, and are taught to respect one's self and not to do drugs. They learn about good medicine that a doctor prescribes, and are told why it is important not to take anybody else's medicine. Unless a child is living with alcoholism in the family, or live in an area where drug use is pervasive, he or she will have no idea what drug use is really about. I wish this were universally true, but it is not. Working with an 11-year-old today is like working with a 14-year-old twenty years ago. Kids are more street-smart today due to the exposure they receive through various media outlets. Young people need to be given strategies like these to help them assess situations they might find themselves in:

- Be a detective—assess the situation.

- Use your eyes and ears.

- See if you can smell trouble—rely on your instincts.

- Begin to think about how to get out of this mess.

- Pick the path you want to go down.

- Think about the consequences that relate to each path.

- Leave.

While these strategies teach young people how to assess a situation and come to a decision, the following strategies/responses are those young people can use when put in an awkward situation such as being asked to smoke a joint or drink some beer:

- "*I said no.*" (stated with confidence, not aggressiveness)

- *"Not for me."* (same as above)

- *"I don't think so."* (same as above)

- *"I do not want to be punished/grounded."* (blame why they cannot participate on somebody else)

- *"I cannot believe you are asking me to do this."*

- *"I thought you were my friend."*

- Make up any excuse that works.

- Use humor.

- *"Let's think of something else to do."*

- Just leave the scene.

I also encourage parents to have a secret code with their kids. There are several different ways to do this:

- *Use a hand signal.* Instead of yelling and screaming, when your child begins to frustrate the heck out of you (yes, I like to use clinical terms when describing behavior), pick a hand signal that your family agrees on. Maybe the signal will be grabbing the side of your face. When your child begins to scream at the mall, get his attention and grab the side of your face, which—interpreted by the child—means *"Get your act together or we are going home."* Yes, believe it or not, I have had parents try this, and for some it worked, for others it was a disaster. If you ever read a self-help book that guarantees results, be very skeptical. Any strategy that I offer has worked with some kids and failed with others.

- *Have a special word or phrase.* This is to be used if your child is in a setup and needs to get out. Jack (not his real name) was dropped off at the mall, and later he was to go to a friend's house to spend the night. When he arrived at his friend's house, he discovered that his friend's older sister was having a few friends over and the parents were out for the evening. When the older kids (10th graders) began to smoke pot out in the back yard and invited Jack and the brother (8th graders) to join them, Jack became uncomfortable. He had never smoked pot and had no intention to start now, but he was stuck. The older kids were cool, and one girl in particular began to talk to Jack and was encouraging him to try it. Jack was now in love. Here he was at a party with high school kids and this girl began to pay attention to him. Jack was not assertive enough or confident enough to just pick up the phone and say "*Pick me up.*" He could not get himself to tell his friend that he was feeling uncomfortable and wanted to go home. Now I know many of you are thinking to yourselves that he should have just called home and left. Okay parents, here are some questions to figure out how assertive you really are?

- A child is picking on other kids in your neighborhood; will you call the parents to let them know about their child's behavior?

- You live in a neighborhood that is about to have a community party at the pool. At your association meeting, you stand up and suggest that no alcohol be served due to younger children being present at the pool. You suggest that there be two parties: one for the kids and one later in the evening for the adults, where alcohol could be served. Would you be willing to do that?

- You hear two kids talking at the bus stop, using profanity in front of some younger children. Would you say anything?

- You hear two parents talking about how they do not like a particular teacher in front of several kids who attend that school where the teacher works. Would you say anything?

- You hang out with other adults you know drink to the point where it changes their behavior. Would you say anything?

Do you see where I am going with this? Peer acceptance is not just a kid thing. It is a people thing. So what decision did Jack make? He told his friend that he had to use the phone to check in; because he told his mom he would call her when he got to his friend's house. His friend stayed in the room with Jack while he used the phone. Jack shared the secret code with his mother and she responded by asking him if he was in trouble. He said "yes" and hung up the phone. Jack told his friend he should not have called home because now he had to leave. It doesn't matter how a child gets himself out of a risky situation, as long as he gets out. Jack was not assertive enough to do it himself; he needed to save face, and he did. Critics of this strategy say that I am teaching kids to lie. They have the right to believe what they want. All I know is that Jack got home safe that night. And that's what matters to me.

- *Share your secret code with your best friend.* Sharon (not her real name) was on a double date set up by her friend with a guy she really wanted to meet. Sharon and her date were in the back seat, while her girlfriend and her boyfriend were in the front seat making out. The boy in the back seat began to make his move, a move that Sharon was not ready for. Sharon needed to get her girl-friend's attention, but wasn't quite sure what to say, so she shared her secret code. The girl in the front seat told her boyfriend she wasn't feeling well and to take them home. He did.

Does a secret code work every time? No, many kids have told me it's lame and it doesn't work. Some kids have said that their friends would never pressure them to do something they didn't want to do. The problem with that statement is that I just don't believe them.

19

Averting Risks, Imposing Consequences

If you have not put a foundation in place by the time your children are in high school and are just now telling them about the dangers of drug use, your role in helping them stay drug-free may be difficult—not impossible, but difficult. Here are some ideas for averting risks and imposing consequences.

When your child says she will be attending a party, or you find out that getting a few friends together means a party:

- Tell them to have fun, but also share your concern (*"Your friends may want you to drink or use other drugs. How will you handle that kind of pressure? I know you don't want to lose your friends, and I'm not saying you will if you don't drink or smoke pot, but the whole thing just scares me."*) Continue on with the rules you have set up for alcohol and other drug use and make sure they know the secret code.

- Your teen might respond by saying, *"Don't worry about me, I will be fine. My friends would never ask me to do something I do not want to do."* Continue anyway.

- Give some examples of how peer pressure impacted your life as a kid and how it impacts your life now as an adult.

- Share *again* your expectations, wants, and needs.

- Role-play if necessary.

- Know who is having the party, what time and where (location and number if possible), with whom your child is going, whether any parents will be home, and whether they will be serving alcohol.

Were you ever pressured to do something you didn't want to do when you were a teen? If so, was it because your friends pressured you, or because you put pressure on yourself because you didn't want to be rejected by your peers or look foolish in front of friends?

If your child does come home under the influence of alcohol or other drugs please try **not** to:

- *Confront your teenager about drinking when they are drunk or high.* Wait until the next day when clearer heads prevail. Restate your expectations and your concerns. Let them know that you want the behavior to stop. Your passion and perception of the problem will drive your intervention strategies. Simply put, if you see it as a problem, you will not tolerate it. You will address it accordingly.

- *Take care of them when they have a hangover.* Let them feel the consequences of their drinking.

- *Make excuses for them.* Do not get into a conversation that begins to justify your child's drug use. *"Everyone is doing it"* is not a reason to use. This is difficult since many parents who went to high school and college remember so many fun and good times they had when they were drunk or stoned. I want you to really think about that statement and how it relates to why so many parents allow their children to drink alcohol. Do you put underage drinking in the same category as other behaviors you would not tolerate? Make a list of those behaviors you do not tolerate in your own kids and see if underage drinking makes the list.

- *Take responsibility for them.* Kids must be responsible for the choices they make.

- *Accept this behavior as normal.* I realize we need to have a paradigm shift when it comes to normalizing behavior. We have come to expect our kids to use alcohol and, in some cases, smoke pot. Unless parents change their perception of the problem, underage drinking will continue.

- *Make threats you cannot back up.* Do not threaten them with consequences that you know will be difficult to enforce. Once the teen figures out that their parents were bluffing, it is difficult for the parent to regain credibility with any consequence they try to implement.

- *Continue to give him/her money or a license* to drive if the using behavior continues.

- *Make them too comfortable.* I know it would be easy to get them to bed, cover them up with a blanket, and then feed them breakfast in bed the next day after they wake up. My point here is to try not to make them too comfortable.

- *Keep them home from school* the next day unless there are legitimate medical reasons to do so.

I realize many of these ideas may be difficult to follow through with, but I believe that kids need to understand the natural consequences that sometimes occur with drug use. It is important that you expect your child not to use, but it is also important to know that other kids may be using and to express your concerns about that. I remember a story I heard many years ago during a seminar, about a father sitting down with his son before handing over the keys to the car. The father writes a letter to the governor stating, *"If my son is found driving around with kids who are using drugs, or my son is using drugs in the car or behind the wheel, I give you permission to pull his license until he is 18 years old."* The father puts the letter in the desk drawer, looks at his son, and says, *"Don't give me a reason to send it."*

I know that some of you who may be reading this book have teenagers who are already beyond the strategies I have suggested. They may already be into the throes of addiction, where their lives have become unmanageable, but they don't see it. You might not see it either, or cannot put yourself in a place to admit it because it is too painful.

My focus for this particular book is on prevention, not intervention, but I would like to share with you some thoughts I offer to parents who are going through difficult times with their teen's drug use. The most difficult decisions parents sometimes have to make involve hospitalizing their child against his will, asking their child to leave the house due to his behavior, leaving their child in jail, pressing charges against their child due to the consequences of his behavior, or setting up an intervention with the intention of implementing one of those strategies. I have met and talked with hundreds of parents who have had to make some of these decisions and they are never easy. Do not let any self-help book, adult, or therapist tell you differently. Every time I talk with a family who feels they have lost their child to drug use, I realize that we could be talking about anybody's kids, mine included. Unless you have had to make one of those decisions as a parent, it may be difficult for you to put yourself in their place. We as parents do the best we can out of love and concern for our kids. Sometimes we do all we can for our kids, and they still make poor choices. Sometimes we make the mistake of not allowing our children to feel the full extent of their consequences from early drug use before it gets out of control. We tell ourselves they are just kids who made mistakes and that we love them and care about them. We bail them out of jail, come to their rescue when they get in trouble in school, allow them to get behind the wheel of a car and pay for their car insurance, knowing that they use alcohol or other drugs. The following are some thoughts I offer parents when the call comes in asking for help:

- If you are married, regardless of how healthy or unhealthy your marriage is, get on the same page in addressing your teenager's drug use. So often intervention fails because parents are not in agreement.

- Many times parents will look at their child as being "the identified patient," thinking that the whole problem lies with the child. You cannot drive a car on three wheels and expect it to work. Regardless of the problem your child is having, understand that it can affect every other person in that house. Sometimes parents think that if their child gets better that the marriage will improve, not realizing that once the child is getting help, problems may remain in the marriage. This is especially true for parents who have children who may be suicidal, depressed, or hostile. Please get some help and support together. Taking that pressure off of the child and acknowledging that everyone is in this together may encourage the teen to go for help.

- Sometimes you may need to talk with someone in the community first before talking to your child about your concerns or taking them for help.

- Do not beat yourselves up for past mistakes. This thinking has no value and will drain what energy you have left in supporting your child.

- Know that what you do for your child is out of care and concern. Kids do get better and they do appreciate the love and support you give them during their time of crisis. They are just not in a position of letting you know that right now.

20

Talking: the First Line of Defense

I want to offer you some strategies that I have shared with parents when they tell me *"I have a son or daughter doing this behavior."* These ideas run the gamut of developmental stages. Some parents will call to let me know the strategy was successful, while others call to let me know the strategy did not work. Then we try something else. Most of these parents have kids who are healthy, but just get stuck at times along the way. Many of these strategies are preventative in nature, in hopes that the concern or issue will not go on to need other or ongoing interventions.

- Give neighbors the permission to report behavior. Here is an example of how you can do that:

Neighborhood Contract
I give permission for my neighbors to call me with any information they see or hear about my child's behavior being inappropriate. I will be open to your call.

Thank you

Parents sign below

- Keep your nose in their business. Always.

- What are your absolutes and what are you willing to negotiate? What are you willing to let go of?

- When you approach your child to talk about serious issues, make sure it is a good time. That goes for your child approaching you as well.

- Sometimes you need a neutral place to talk.

- Have your child explain what they are asking for in writing if you don't have the time to talk or can't understand what they are trying to say.

- If you say, "*Let me get back to you,*" make sure you do it.

- Talk to your child about not asking for something in front of their friends.

- Go ahead and take a time out if you need one.

- If you have a tendency to have screaming matches with your teen (or for that matter, your 5th grader), tape your conversation and play it back later.

- If your child wants you to just listen to her, then do it. I know it can be very difficult to just give your full attention and listen without giving any feedback, any advice, comments, or judgments. After she is finished talking, and she asks you for some advice, (she may not) help her with open-ended questions like, "*Have you thought about…?*" or "*I'm not sure if this will work, but have you tried…?*" This puts the onus of taking responsibly for her decisions back on her, and builds up her confidence in thinking for herself. (**visit Appendix D Tips For Teens, for teens who want to help their friends through a problem they may be having)**

- Send a letter. Some parents have a difficult time with words in sharing how they feel about their child. Sometimes sending a letter in the mail expressing how proud you are of them can do wonders for a teen's self-esteem. I have had several parents do this with great success.

- Keep them busy, but make sure they have some down time. Help them create that balance. We all could use a little down time.

- Cross gender. Have mom spend some time with the son alone and dad with his daughter. Let them plan the hour, half-day, or day once in a while. No strategy can replace time spent with your kids.

- Give your kids only as much information as they need to know about your past drug use or sexual activity. How much they need to know depends on the situation and your knowledge of your kids.

- Practice problem solving in front of your kids. If you and your husband have a simple conflict that does not involve the kids, practice this problem solving skill and then use this in front of the kids. If you are a single parent, do this with a friend or relative. Remember, make sure it is a problem that is solvable.

- Define the problem.

- Check out each other's feelings in regards to the problem (put yourself in their shoes).

- Brainstorm for possible solutions.

- Choose a solution that fits.

- Put your child in the position of being the expert once in a while.

You can never have enough ideas when it comes to working with kids. Prevention is an odds game. My goal is to put off the average age of first-time everything for as long as I possibly can.

Rules of the Road

One issue that comes up at almost every high school party is who is going to drive kids home if they are wasted. I was in a car accident once and will spare you the details, but I was the designated driver. Being in that seat can be as dangerous as or more dangerous than being the person who is drunk or high in the back seat. Here are my two guidelines for designated drivers. I will tell you now that most teens do not like either one:

- Teens should not be designated drivers. Only if everything else fails should they be designated to take one teen home at a time, safely buckled in the back seat, with adult permission. Another sober teen should go with them, and should be seated next to the person they are taking home.

- An adult should be called to escort one to two teens home at a time, both in the back seat, and both buckled in. If possible, it might be helpful to have another adult with you, depending on the situation. Be smart. Fathers should not attempt to take teenage girls home alone unless they have another adult with them, preferably a female adult or his kids. I would encourage moms to do the same. It may sound like overkill, but these are the times we live in.

One of Many Quick Lessons Taught to Me by Kids

It is very difficult today to tell who is using drugs and who is not. I was waiting to meet with a principal once, when three students walked in and sat down. I started up a conversation and wanted to know what was going on in the school, since I was unfamiliar with the community. I asked them about the students' drugs of choice and their perception of who used and who didn't. A student had just died, which is the reason I was there. Many of the students were praying by the time I walked downstairs and involved in some kind of prayer chain. The students began pointing out several students to me whom they said were some of the biggest drug users in the school. They said that their parents didn't know, because they thought their kids were safe being in a youth group. At a leadership conference, a junior in high school told me she had never drank or seen pot before in her life until band camp. Both of these incidents may be isolated, but the point is well taken.

As parents, we cannot become complacent and think our kids are safe just because they are involved in faith-based activities or activities we normally would not associate with drug use. So how many high school teens are actually doing drugs? Most research will tell you anywhere from 20 percent to 40 percent, depending on the study, the drug you are talking about, the frequency, and how the data is collected and reported. Most teens would tell you that almost everybody parties. The truth lies somewhere in the middle.

The bottom line is, if kids are using in the community the school sits in, it is likely that kids in the school are using drugs. We seem to focus too much on how many kids are using drugs and not enough on the kids who aren't. We seem to be fixated on bringing in recovering kids who tell their personal stories in hopes of discouraging others not to use. This can be very powerful and some kids need to hear their stories, but what about bringing in kids who don't use and find out from them what keeps them drug-free?

So, Where Do We Go From Here?

In chapter 3 we talked about having a code of ethics. Within this code can be your "no-use" message. Research has shown that a "no-use" message repeated consistently and over time, along with parents having unfavorable attitudes towards drug use, can become a protective factor. (Hawkins and Catalino, risk and protective factor research) So what does this mean? I do not care if you choose to have a glass of wine with dinner or a few beers while you are watching a game. Alcohol is legal for adults and it is your decision how much you want to consume or not consume. But I would ask you to consider this. When you have your adult friends over on a Friday or Saturday night, serve alcohol or any other refreshment you like. But the next week, serve everything but alcohol. Your children need to understand that how you socialize and relate to your friends does not revolve around alcohol. Simply stated, you can have fun and relax without alcohol. Your kids know the difference between a parent who drinks and a parent who drinks excessively by 4th or 5th grade. My battle is not with kids under 11 years of age (whether they are going to drink or not); instead it is the parents of many of these children who have crossed the line into addictive behavior, and will not acknowledge it or get help. I have spoken to more than 20,000 kids under the age of 11 who are asked to raise their hands if they have someone in their life that drinks alcohol to the point where it changes their behavior, and they are concerned about them. For every 100 kids, I will see 10 to 20 hands go up. Most of these kids will come to me in private to share that they were talking about a parent. **Alcohol misuse impacts so many people and yet many adults still do not consider alcohol a drug.**

We must keep things in perspective if we are to change the norm. There are many parent and community groups doing wonderful things with little money. Many of these groups are trying to impact underage drinking by bringing together law enforcement, government and community agencies to put pressure on liquor establishments—through education and spot checks—so that these establishments will not sell alcohol to minors. Kids are responsible for the choices they make, but underage drinking is an adult problem that needs to be addressed by adults. There are many parents today who still provide alcohol to their kids. There are many parents today who still provide alcohol for their kids' parties. Kids can get alcohol from older siblings, from talking an adult into buying it for them, by using fake IDs, and often from their parents. It is important for parents and adults to change our attitudes and perceptions about alcohol and pot, but we also have to change our behaviors. We must realize that alcohol is a drug that can be most harmful to a person under the age of 21. We must remember also that there have been numerous studies over the last 20 years that link alcohol misuse to crime, accidents, and poor academic performance.

The good news is that there are more teens today than in recent decades involved in community service, peer programs, and who genuinely want to make a difference in their communities. We just don't hear about them very much. I had a father call me several years ago, telling me that his son came home upset because he could not find anyone to go out with Saturday night. He was choosing not to do drugs and couldn't find any drug-free friends. I know those kids are out there, and so do you. I will admit to thinking that everyone in high school back in the early 70s drank alcohol or smoked pot. Many years ago, I was asked to do a workshop on drug perception and I decided to revisit my senior class pictures. I went back to my high school yearbook, and really looked at the pictures of my graduation class to see who was using, who was rumored to be using, and who I knew for sure was not using. My feeling about everybody who was using had changed. My perception was wrong. What does your high school senior class look like in terms of drug use? I encourage you to take another look.

Many of us who were teenagers in the 60s, 70s, or 80s listened to music that was full of drug references. One day many years ago, I was lying around listening to music when a song came on that I had never heard before. I can't believe they would just play a song that would chant the words *"everybody must get stoned,"* written by Bob Dylan. It sounded pretty cool back then. I guess now that I'm a parent, it doesn't sound so cool anymore.

If you need to be reminded that not all high school kids drink or use other drugs, or you are beginning to lose faith in kids today, please read this letter I received:

Dear Neighbors:

I just wanted to inform you that my friend and I are having a rather large New Year's Eve party this evening. We are expecting lots of people and some music. Other than that, we will not tolerate any drinking, smoking, or anything of the sort. If anything should disturb you, feel free to call my house. My parents will be home at all times, and will not let anything stupid occur. Some kids will be spending the night, so there may be some cars on the street overnight. (Ninety-nine percent of our guests will be band students under 18, so I do not expect any trouble.) Thank you for your consideration, and have a happy New Year.

I found this in my mailbox the day of the party. The only disappointment was that I wasn't invited.

21

Sex in Music

I was in a record store the other day looking for CDs. There in a bin in the front, sat a CD I just could not believe would be sitting out in view for everyone to see. I was thankful my kids were not with me. There comes a time when you think you've seen and heard it all. For years, bands have introduced themselves to the consumer through provocative names and suggestive artwork on the cover of the album or CD, including the infamous Beatles' butcher baby album cover (banned almost immediately) and the Guns N' Roses album cover image (initially banned because adults felt it promoted sexual assault, but eventually moved to the inside sleeve). Bands understand that the names and images they choose make a statement about who and what they represent. These are the first things that attract us to a band or artist we may not know. This is especially true for death metal bands. The cover of the CD I saw in the store would still make most adults stop in their tracks out of disbelief. Most parents would not buy this CD based on the band's name alone. Many teenagers would pick it up and buy it just for the cover. Who is this band? What would be the point in me telling you? The band is rather obscure, but does have a strong following for those who like this particular type of music. Their music is not played on the radio, and you would not find their songs on any Billboard Top 100. Kids find out about bands like this the way we did, by word of mouth. If the band is talented, it will increase its following, which is what happened to Metallica, a band that relatively few people knew. Word spread about this band throughout the country and the world because kids related to them, but their music initially was not played on the radio. Today, you can hear them on almost any radio station that plays rock 'n roll and they are a mainstream band for kids who listen to metal.

The mistake some adults make, however good their intentions are, is to go after a band that has an outrageous act, strong anti-faith message, gratuitous violence, or sexual themes in their music. It would make more sense to address particular themes being presented to our youth in music today, rather than singling out one or two bands. As I've said before, if the band is not popular but has a small following, bringing attention to the band increases the odds that more kids will buy the CDs and listen to the music out of curiosity or rebellion.

Even if the band is popular and relates to kids, taking on the band is no guarantee that kids will stop listening to them. Alice Cooper is a perfect example of this. Many of us grew up listening to Alice Cooper against everyone's wishes, and most kids stuck with Alice because they felt they could relate to his music. I am not endorsing or supporting any particular band, but I am suggesting that most kids, just like us when we were young, are able to differentiate between the bands they like and those they don't. If we want a child to stop listening to a particular type of music, we must work at getting them to understand what it is about the message that the artist is trying to send that is offensive. Maybe the artist's particular lifestyle offends the family's code of ethics. Whatever the case may be, that is every parent's choice to make. Today, Alice Cooper seems tame compared to other acts that go much further than just chopping off the head of a mannequin. We do have the right to protest. We do have the right to protect our kids. But we are also not alone. Many teenagers feel the same way most adults do about some of the music and lyrics we are exposed to today. The same thing can be said for media influences. Hundreds of kids will tell me that they think lyrics and movies impact peoples' thinking and behavior. We must choose our power struggles carefully, and be ready to look at ourselves first before we put ourselves in a position of making judgments. It is sad that our kids are being pushed to grow up so fast. I have seen 4th and 5th grade girls become upset because they do not look like the girls on the covers of the magazines they see at the checkout counter at the local grocery store. I have 4th and 5th grade boys beginning to react the same way to images of men who have tight abs and muscles. Who wouldn't want that? Many sport magazines also have pictures of beautiful women in bathing suits or partially clothed. What does that have to do with sports? What do you think they are selling? Take a look at the magazine racks and keep track of how many covers you see that are selling sex. Walk into a comic store, and look at the covers on the comic books to see how women are being represented. The point I'm trying to make is that the prevalence of sexual images in the media is driven by adults. Many of us watch the soaps on TV, we buy the magazines with the provocative covers, and we support the movies and the television shows that may involve explicit sexual content. So it should not be a surprise to any of us that our kids want to talk about sex.

22

Decoding the Messages in Music

I have read different articles that attempted to analyze the Beatles' song, "Why Don't We Do It In The Road?" What do you think it means? Please choose one of the following answers:

- Changing a tire

- Nothing

- Drug use

- Having sex

Yes, changing a tire would be a safe bet. We have gone from "Why Don't We Do It In The Road", to "L.G.B.N.A.F." by Ice-T (Let's Get Butt Naked and F**k), in just 35 years. One song alludes to a certain kind of behavior, where the other one leaves nothing to the imagination, just straight-up and in-your-face sex. Alanis Morissette talks about a woman scorned in her hit song, "You Oughta Know", which came out a few years ago. Alanis is very explicit when letting you know how she feels. I've talked to several women who could identify with what Alanis was trying to communicate to her listeners. The interesting point is that this song received enormous airplay, received acolytes, and rose to the top of the charts along with the CD called "Jagged Little Pill." It truly was the first pop radio song I could remember that used profanity so openly. A woman scorned in the 60s, say, Lesley Gore in the song, "It's My Party", expressed her sadness by letting people know "*[she] can cry if [she] want[s] to*" because someone left with somebody they weren't supposed to. Many of us can relate to that song and others like it, because we have been there before.

"*I can't live without you,*" "*I need a man to make it through,*" or "*I will change who I am for you*" were common themes. Not anymore. This new breed of female artists, like Ani Difranco, is made up of independent women. Difranco sings

81

about domestic violence and other issues that relate to women in hopes of pulling them out of the role of being a victim. Groups like TLC and En Vogue look to empower women, a far cry from 40 years ago. (Of course, these performers were influenced by Patti Smith, Chrissie Hynde, Pat Benatar, Debbie Harry, Tina Turner and many other strong female artists.) But attitudes were different then. What radio stations found to be offensive material years ago can now be seen on PBS. Something else that has changed in the past 40 years is that people of all ages listen to all types of music. I can be stopped at a light in my car and the cars on both sides of me can be listening to the same type of music. The difference is the car to my left has a 16-year-old driving it, while the car to my right has a 51-year-old behind the wheel. Many parents today listen to the same music their kids do. I have 30-, 40-, and 50-year-old friends who still attend concerts and keep up with the latest sounds. Did your parents attend the Led Zeppelin concert with you? Did you bring your parents to see the Clash? Did you bring them to see Public Enemy? There is still some disagreement, though, when it comes to taste in music. Most parents do not like the gratuitously violent lyrics in most rap and metal songs. There will always be genres of music that parents won't like.

I was talking to a group of teenagers about the messages some rap music sends about women. I asked the girls to put their name in place of the words "b***h" or "ho" and see if the song took on a different meaning. Here is what they had to say:

- *"I am not like that."*

- *"They are not talking about me."*

- *"They are talking about those girls who slut around."*

- *"They are not talking about all women."*

- *"It's a little strange to see my name in a song that is followed by the words 'f**k' and 'big d**k,' but I still know they're not talking about me. Don't ask my mother to do this activity."*

I asked them if they were mothers, would they allow their daughters to listen to this music? They all said "no." I asked them if their mothers could stop them from listening to certain kinds of music and their response was "no." "We could just leave the house and listen to it somewhere else." I asked them if their daughters did that, would that be showing respect? "*No*," they responded. There was a moment of silence and than one girl spoke up and said, "*Hey, wait a minute, you're confusing us!"* "*No, I'm not trying to confuse you,*" I said. "*I'm just getting you to look at this from a different perspective.*"

I had a similar experience when I was asked to do a panel about the impact (if any) that lyrics had on youth. The band on the panel with me had been banned in three countries due to their outrageous act and song lyrics. The audience could not wait to meet the band. I was a sheep being thrown to the wolves. Once again, I knew it would be a set-up, but I felt strongly that the perspective gained was something I could go on to share with other parents. It was a very difficult gig to do. One of the songs I asked the audience about was a song that had to do with domestic violence. A woman who is pregnant is thrown down the stairs. I would say that most women in the audience supported the band in stating that the song was fiction. "*There are women who drive their men f**king nuts, and this song is really about what some men wish they could do, but would never do. Isn't it better to bring it out in fantasy as opposed to reality?*" What do you think? In order to begin our discussion about sex and differences, I have some questions I want you to think about:

- Who taught you the most about being a woman?

- Who taught you the most about being a man?

- Were you allowed to date as a teenager?

- Were you asked to wait until marriage to have sex?

- Was sex talked about in your house growing up?

- Could you talk about anything or were there rules about what you could talk about?

Kids can form opinions about each of the above questions just by listening to music, watching TV, watching movies, reading print, or surfing the Web. They can also learn about these things from each other. If kids do not get their questions answered—and their needs met—through you, they will find what they need somewhere else.

23

Discussing Difficult Subjects

I was asked to do a workshop with middle school parents outside of the school, to address ways parents can talk to their kids about difficult subjects. I wanted to make parents comfortable with one another, so we introduced ourselves and did some sharing. A woman started the conversation with the comment, *"My son, who is in 6ᵗʰ grade, heard that several kids were caught having oral sex in the neighborhood. I know he wanted to discuss it more, but I just wasn't sure where to go with it."* And we were off. Here are some ideas in talking to your kids about sensitive subject matters:

- *Be clear about what you believe.* Have insight about your position before discussing it with your kids.

- *Role-play with other adults.* I have had several parents share with me that talking about it with another adult was helpful.

- *Anticipate questions.* During your role-play, think one question ahead. Most kids will build one question into the next. Many middle and high school kids will ask their parents to personalize the question, just like they do with the drug question. They'll ask, *"Have you ever had oral sex? Have you ever done drugs?"* Other kids are too embarrassed to ask their parents personal questions about sex.

- *Use the three As: acknowledgement, acceptance, approval.* When talking about difficult subjects, use the three As. For example, homosexuality is a sensitive topic for people to talk about, and most people are very passionate about where they stand on the topic. Wherever you stand on the topic, be open to the three As.

  - *Acknowledgement.* Can you name three popular TV shows with a main character who is gay or subject matter that pertains to a gay lifestyle? I remember watching *Buffy the Vampire Slayer* recently, and somewhere in the middle of the show, Willow, who is a character on the show, kissed another female character—not a peck, a long deep kiss. I ran downstairs and called a friend of mine whom I know watches the show every week, and their daughter (who is in 8th grade) answered the phone. I asked her if she watched the show tonight and she said, "*Yes, I thought it was good.*" I was waiting for her to make a comment, or ask me a question in hopes of getting a rise out of me. Nothing. She was completely unaffected by it all. Ten years ago, everyone would have been talking about it. We must acknowledge that different lifestyles exist in our society today. Acknowledgement does not mean approval.

- *Acceptance.* A young man who was openly gay was being bullied by a group of kids because he was gay. I've worked with several kids over the years who were bullied simply because they were overweight, Jewish, Christian, Latino, gothic, and so on. Many boys are bullied if they don't fit the boy box. I recall a young 5th-grade boy in particular who liked traditionally feminine colors, liked to dance, and was not good at sports. Several boys took it upon themselves to call him gay, which started around the third grade, and they made his life so miserable that he didn't want to ride the bus or go to school anymore. He was a nice kid who was a bit different from the norm. What is it about people who differ from the norm that scares us so much? Accepting people who are different does not mean approval. Acceptance means allowing people the right to live in freedom without persecution. Isn't that what we all are trying to teach our kids? Sometimes we as parents find it difficult to accept our own kids for the same reasons other kids reject them—because they are different or just don't fit into the norm. Many parents are embarrassed if their son wants to take dance lessons as opposed to playing baseball, or if their daughter would rather play football than dance. More and more, parents are proud of their daughters for being athletic, and it's becoming more accepted for girls to explore outside of gender roles. While we have become more flexible and encouraging about girls being involved in all sorts of activities, we still hold boys to strict gender roles in terms of what we allow them to get involved in. Remember that whatever stereotypes and attitudes we hold about how girls and boys should behave and activities they should be involved with trickle down to our children. Let the boys dance and let the girls play football. Who creates the rules and puts limitations on what our boys and girls are allowed to play and get involved in? Who normalizes behavior, and who suffers the consequences of those norms?

- *Approval.* Acknowledgement and acceptance are things I believe every parent should teach their kids in the context of what I am talking about here.

However, when it comes down to approval, it is every parent's decision how they choose to share their morals and values with their kids. Once again, you can acknowledge that a behavior or lifestyle exists, you can accept that it is a part of our culture and society today, but it is your choice whether you approve of it or not.

- *Acknowledge your feelings.* Admit to your child that you are a little uncomfortable with the subject matter. Here is a formula that may be helpful (example of a daughter approaching her father):

  - *"I feel"*—Insert your feeling word (*"uncomfortable"*).

  - *"Talking about"*—State the subject matter (*"boys"*).

  - *"So can you"*—State the action you desire (*"go to your mother?"*).

- *Remember the basics.* All of the above topics that we are talking about here are probably planted somewhere in the foundation that you have set for your kids. Come from that perspective when talking about sensitive topics.

- *Allow for disagreement.* Realize that your child or spouse may disagree with your view.

- *Present the facts.* Present accurate information along with values and beliefs.

- *Keep up with sexual culture.* Most kids find oral sex okay, and do not consider it sex.

- *Don't make assumptions.* Do not assume your child is into a certain behavior by the questions he or she is asking.

- *Ask for help.* Get help from a relative, clergy, or trusted friend if you are unwilling to talk about certain issues with your kids. It is better that they get the information from somebody you trust, as opposed to somebody you do not know.

24

Assessing Relationships

In working with high school students in leadership settings, we always seem to get into conversations about relationships. The first things we talk about are leadership qualities and emotional maturity. Here is a list that students helped me develop in defining what *leadership* and *emotional maturity* involve:

- Flexibility

- Healthy manipulation

- Understanding

- Acknowledgement, acceptance, approval

- Reliability

- Communication

- Empathy

- Moderation and balance

- Sincerity

- Follow-through

- Ability to listen more than talk

- Questioning more than stating

- Assertiveness and self-confidence

- Ability to admit when wrong

- Honesty

- Capacity to love

- Ability to manage anger appropriately

- Sense of humor

- Ability to look for ways of connecting

- Strong boundaries

- Knowledge of limits

- Having a set of long- and short-term goals

- Understanding there are positive and negative consequences to behavior and decisions that we make in life.

Healthy and Unhealthy Relationships

When I talk to high school kids about relationships, I ask them if they would like to focus on siblings, friends, parents or boyfriend/girlfriend relationships. Most want to talk about boyfriend/girlfriend relationships, so we start with healthy and unhealthy relationships.

Characteristics of a *healthy* relationship:

- You are allowed to change your mind.

- You can be yourself.

- You are respected.

- You can say no.

- You give and receive.

- You are safe and trusted.

- You can agree to disagree.

- You can keep spending time with your friends.

- You don't have to be with each other all the time (you have that choice).

- If you have sex or had sex, you can stop.

- You do not put each other in unhealthy situations.

- You support and encourage each other.

- You lift each other up, as opposed to bringing each other down.

Qualities of an *unhealthy* relationship:

- Relationship involves alcohol or other drug use.

- One person is possessive.

- One person has a lot of rage.

- One person loses his/her temper easily.

- One person has *excessive* mood swings.

- One person is controlling.

- One person is *extremely* jealous.

- One person constantly puts the other down or is verbally abusive.

- One person chooses friends for the other person.

- One person tells the other person how to dress.

- One person pressures the other to have sex.

- One person uses manipulation to get his/her way on a consistent basis.

I remember one evening getting ready to do a workshop for parents on healthy peer relationships, when I spotted a mother walking towards me. She was gasping for air as she approached the stage and asked if we could talk for a few minutes. I had been at the high school earlier in the day talking with high school students about relationships. She shared that she was grateful for the support and encouragement I gave her daughter. I had no idea what she was talking about. Her daughter was in an abusive relationship and refused to break up with her boyfriend. Mother began describing her daughter's relationship with this boy. Here is a profile of what the relationship looked like. Do you know anyone who is in a relationship like this?

- Her boyfriend drank and occasionally used other drugs.

- He did not approve of the way she dressed or wore her make up even though that is what attracted him to her in the first place.

- He had a short temper and lacked patience.

- Because they went to different schools, he made her carry a cell phone in case he needed her.

- She had to stop spending time with her friends.

- He made most of the decisions in the relationship.

The mother shared that her daughter stayed because she loves him and thinks she can change him. Why is it that women think they can change men and men think women will never change? The mother said that her daughter was still seeing her boyfriend, but is hopeful that will change in the near future. She gave me a hug, thanked me for listening, and began to walk away. I stopped her and said, "*I am so sorry, but I don't know your daughter. You must have me mistaken with somebody else.*" She asked if I talked to high school kids today and I said, "*Yes, about 200 kids.*" She responded that her daughter had come home from school crying and was now ready to talk with a counselor. You just never know when something is going to stick. Does information alone change behavior? Let's hope it did today.

Sexual Pressure

During the last part of the workshop with kids, we talk about what to do if you are ever pressured to have sex. When I ask teenagers if they have friends who were ever pressured to have sex, many of them will raise their hands. In this particular group, it was now time to do some role-plays. One role-play in particular always seems to surprise them. Two high school seniors, who have been going out for over a year, talk about taking their relationship to the next level. One student is leaving to go out of state to attend college. That student wants to solidify their relationship by having sex. The student who is leaving must use all that he or she can think of to convince the other student to have sex. The response lines are as follows:

- *"Respect my decision to wait."*

- *"Let me think it over."*

- *"Let me talk to my parents."*

- *"Why is it your way or no way?"*

- *"It goes against my religion!"*

- *"I am saving myself!"*

- *"This goes against my values!"*

- *"I'm sorry you can't wait, I can!"*

- *"I am not ready for that!"*

The surprise is that, in this case, the girl is pressuring the boy. Boys tell me all the time about the pressures they feel when it comes to girls. I remember a group of 9th-grade students at a leadership training saying, *"I bet you wish you were in middle school today."* I asked why, and their comment was *"because the 8thgrade girls are crazy."* To think that boys are not being pressured into having sex at times is a myth. Many of them approach me after a workshop and have story after story about times they felt pressured to have sex. They share that when they do feel pressure to have sex, they have few outlets to talk about it. One young man who was being pressured by his girlfriend, tried to talk to his teammates about it, but they laughed at him and said, *"She is hot; I can't believe you don't want to have sex with her—what are you, gay?"*

No, he was not gay. He just was not ready to have sex. Many parents of middle and high school boys tell me how their son's phone rings at all hours of the night and how aggressive girls have become making advances to the boys. The role-play is a good experience for both sexes to go through, because it allows them to see and feel the pressure to have sex from different perspectives. It also allows them to practice using refusal skills in a safe environment. Role-playing really helps prepare kids for situations they may find themselves in later in life.

New Responsibilities

Adults often ask me what has changed when it comes to kids and sex. Today, it is much more difficult to shelter kids from the exposure they receive from ads, billboards, beer commercials, sitcoms, movies, music, and the internet. Having a **Code of Ethics**, teaching your children **Media Literacy**, and keeping your computer with internet connection in a family room will help limit some of the exposure. I encourage you to have an **Internet Safety Contract** that both you and your kids sign before they are hooked up to the internet.

One way to create an online safety contract is as follows:

1. Let us know when something or someone makes you feel uncomfortable.

2. Let us know if someone is asking you for personal information.

3. We know there are times inappropriate messages or pictures will appear on the screen, let us know when this happens as it happens to us as well.

4. Staying safe means keeping your password and buddy list (friends) to yourself.

5. We have heard of young people who create websites about people they do not like. We know this is something you would not take part in. Let us know if you are being asked to take part in such a website, e-mail, text message, or instant message that includes putting someone down and disrespecting them. This type of message goes against our code of ethics.

Please sign this agreement that states you will be a responsible internet user and will come to us with any of the issues or challenges stated above.

For more information visit www.missingkids.com or type internet safety contract into any search engine for more ideas.

No matter how many safety blocks you have, pop-up ads or pornographic sites seem to appear out of nowhere. There are certain catchwords that can bring unwanted sites to your computer screen without your child doing anything wrong. Words like "teasing," "management," "stress," and "discipline" will bring up unwanted sites at times. I am no expert on internet safety, but what I do know is that we must educate ourselves to keep up with our children, if we are going to be effective in minimizing what they see and how they communicate electronically. We have only scratched the surface with technology. The possibilities that technology has to offer us are exciting and at times frightening. We are all in for one wild ride.

Long before the Internet, the music many of us listened to 30 years ago introduced us to sexuality before many of our parents talked with us about it in our own homes. I remember being introduced to "Lola" by the Kinks and finding out at the end of the song that Lola was a man. Do you remember that song? What was your reaction? Songs like "Bobby Brown", by Frank Zappa, that used profanity were written more than 25 years ago. Led Zeppelin wrote "The Lemon Song", more than 30 years ago, and had a line that went: "*Squeeze my lemon, 'til the juice runs down my leg.*" Do you think they were talking about eating fruit in bed? Talking about these songs surprises most adults. Many did not realize that music like this existed in the 70s. Rap was not the first genre of music to talk about sex or to use profanity in its lyrics.

Yes, things have changed. There is no point in quoting dozens of songs, showing you in graphic detail all the words that exist in music today. You know things have changed because we have changed. We as adults are responsible for the changes taking place today on TV, at the movies, on the radio, talk radio and in the music. We have allowed it to come this far.

Some things have not changed, however. Somewhere, some place, there is a parent telling their son or daughter to turn it down. We need to be saying "*Turn it up; let's talk about it. Let's talk about what the words are saying and ask how this fits into our code of ethics.*"

25

Bullying Behavior and Tolerance

"Jeremy spoke in class today…try to erase this from the blackboard…"

"Jeremy", Pearl Jam

Before we begin this chapter, here are some questions to ask yourself and your son or daughter:

- Were you ever picked on as a child?

- Were you ever bullied to the point of not wanting to go to school?

- Did you ever tease or pick on somebody?

- Did you ever bully someone?

- Do you know the difference between teasing and bullying?

- Do you think it is okay for someone to walk away from a fight?

- Do you think sometimes people deserve to be hit?

- Do you have a hard time accepting people who may be different from you?

- Do you think that some of the most popular kids in your school are also the bullies?

- Can teasing ever turn into bullying behavior?

I have worked with many young people who listen to very aggressive music who were also being picked on or bullied. Many of these kids are in special education classes for a variety of reasons. Others are target or gifted kids who, once taken out of their comfort zone, lack some of the same social skills that many of our Special Ed kids lack. Many of them have shared with me that the music offers them some sense of empowerment and control, which seems to be lacking in many of their lives. Many times these kids bully others and then, in return, are bullied, which results in a shameful experience that has a way of repeating itself. Songs like "Jeremy," about a young man who is bullied and then takes his own life, have become a way for me to talk to parents about the issue of teasing and bullying.

Chris' Story

About a year ago I walked into a used CD store and was greeted by a young man sitting behind the counter. He was drawing comic-like figures and listening to a band called Avenged Sevenfold, which fits somewhere between the metal and hardcore genre. I had never heard of the band. I commented on his drawing and shared with him my love of comics and asked him if he owned any comic books. He shared that he had thousands of comics and wanted to sell most of them, but that the majority of them were from the 80s, and that I probably would not be interested. The conversation quickly shifted from comics to music. I wanted to learn more about the hardcore scene, and I knew Chris would be able to help me. Chris looked like someone who had been through the drug scene in the 80s, and was possibly into the darkest part of the hardcore genre. I assumed this based on the comics he read and drew and the tattoos that went up and down his arms. I assumed many things about Chris and wanted to find out more about him, so I asked for a brief interview. As it turned out, all of my assumptions were wrong.

Chris is 28 years old and used to run a Fanzine paper with his best friend called *The Little Demon*. The paper started in 1995 as a comic book with some CD reviews and band interviews. Chris and his friend decided to devote the whole issue to music, courting record labels, and interviewing a wide range of bands. Chris has interviewed hundreds of bands and now supports several bands by doing some artwork and promotional items. I wanted to know from Chris the role music played in his life growing up, and if the music had any influence over decisions he made. Here is what he had to say:

"My early influences were whatever my parents were playing on the radio at the time. Elvis and oldies seemed to be playing a lot in my house. I started to listen to the Fat Boys and Roxanne when I was about eight years old. They were popular at the time. It was in 5th or 6th grade

when I heard a band called Iron Maiden, and, for a variety of reasons, that band, along with the metal genre, spoke to me. My parents trusted me and allowed me to listen to whatever I wanted. They just did not want me listening to music that had profanity in it. I never wanted to disappoint my parents, especially my mother, who to this day I have an open relationship with. We can talk about anything and still do.

"I think people misunderstand me. I realize because of my image, most people think I am a Satan worshipper or use drugs. It's kind of funny. When I am playing jazz in the store, which is a genre of music I like very much, adults will come in and talk to me like I am a real person, but if I play hardcore or death metal in the store, they run to protect their children and say very little to me while they are purchasing CDs." (Many people are afraid of what they do not understand. Much hardcore and death metal sounds like the voices are coming from the bowels of hell. It is loud and most people cannot make out the lyrics. Volume, power, incomprehensible lyrics, and messages that most adults don't get are what make this attractive to kids.)

"My image in high school was very similar to what it is now. I had long hair, and listened to metal, so many kids and adults assumed the worst. Academically, I was not very successful. I was teased and bullied a lot and had very few friends. I spent almost all my time alone. To all those kids who are being picked on I say, 'Find something you love to do and stick with it. You will find your niche. I did.'

"Actually, I had thousands of friends. My music and my comics became my rock and my passion. Outwardly, the image I projected was very different from who I really was. I could listen to the music and live vicariously through what the band was saying. If they were saying 'go and worship the devil,' they would do that. I didn't have to. If they were using drugs, I didn't have to; I would just experience it through the band. Most adults and kids thought I was using drugs in high school; the truth is I didn't drink alcohol until I was 21. No drug use at all. I think that goes back to not wanting to disappoint my parents, especially my mother. I look forward to starting college in the spring. I am going back to take up graphic design. I hope to do artwork for bands." The store was beginning to get crowded so I had to wrap up.

I asked Chris if he felt that the music could influence those kids who may not have that parental support system. His response was "Why don't they have that? If their child is consumed with listening to music that has gratuitous violence, sex, and drug use for hours upon hours, where are the parents during this time? Where is the supervision? Why are the kids so consumed?"

Chris wants to be judged by his character, not his earrings, music, or tattoos, but understands along with his image comes the anticipated criticism and looks that he gets from some adults.

I never did get to ask Chris if he found the aggressive messages in the music he listened to empowering, since he felt a sense of powerlessness to do anything about the kids who were picking on him. Maybe those kids who were picking on him were not worth his effort. What do you think his answer would be?

Maybe his answer would be similar to Hatebreed's answer in the song "You're Never Alone": *"You can't be burdened by your lack of control. Never stray from the path you have chosen."*

Children who are bullied need five things to help them get through the difficult times:

- They need a strong family support system in place.

- They need at least one best friend who they can talk to about anything.

- They need another adult outside of the immediate family who believes in them.

- They need some bystanders to help support them during difficult times.

- They need faith in either themselves or a higher power that they will make it through.

The problem is that many of the kids who most need help may have only one of these types of supports, and some have none. I think it is important for all kids to understand the following:

- Everyone may not like you.

- Everyone may not want to be your friend.

- You may be left out at times.

- You will find friends who will accept you for who you are.

- You are unique and special.

A Brief Look at the Differences Between Teasing and Bullying

I am very passionate about this topic, as I know so many of you are. So many adults who were bullied as kids can be brought back in time to the place the bullying occurred and the people involved just by asking them the question, "*Were you ever bullied?*" We all have an opinion about this topic because we all have contributed to the process. Each of us has been or continues to be a bully, a bystander, or a target. To understand what bullying behavior is, we must first define teasing behavior.

***Teasing* is acceptable when:**

- We use teasing and roasting as a way of fitting in or talking to our friends and everyone involved is getting an equal share of the teasing. (Kids are not ganging up on one person.)

- People are not making fun of someone's disabilities, ethnicity, faith, or other characteristics that are out of the person's control.

- The teasing is not repeated over and over again. It is one thing to be called short, but it is another to be called short on a daily basis. That gets old.

- It is not meant to harm you in any way, and if you asked the person to stop, they would.

- It is done by someone you have a close relationship with. There is always the possibility friends can take teasing too far and end up in a fight, but usually bullying is not involved.

Bullying behavior occurs when these three characteristics are present:

1. **There is a pattern of behavior established.** An example of bullying behavior is saying mean and hurtful things to one person or several people on purpose and for no reason at all. This may include making threatening comments or actions toward one or more. I realize that *mean* and *hurtful* words and interpreting *threatening* comments and *actions* are subjective. What is *mean* and *threatening* to one young person may not be to another. The important concept here to remember is establishing a pattern of behavior. A child who takes another child's milk at lunch and pretends to drink it and won't give it back, might just be being a jerk. Bystanders or an adult

needs to intervene at that point. There is no school policy for kids who are just "acting like a jerk". However, if this behavior continues, or this child begins to do things to a number of students, then a pattern of behavior can be established.

2. **The bullying behavior has a negative impact on the target\victim.**

3. **An imbalance of power is established**. An imbalance of power occurs when a person feels threatened by someone's words or actions and their perception is that they won't be able to protect themselves. We must believe the young persons perception if we as adults are going to help them.

I encourage parents to be pro-active and prepare their children for the possibility that they will be inappropriately teased at some point in their life. Scott Cooper, author of *Sticks and Stones,* discusses ways in which kids can verbally stick up for themselves through the use of scripts. Below are some word phrases that I teach kids to use if they ever find themselves in a situation where they need to verbally stick up for themselves. It is important to remember that these words and phrases will take on different meanings dependant upon the tone of voice and body language used. If the inappropriate teasing has crossed over into bullying behavior as defined above, then an intervention will be needed to see that the bullying behavior comes to an end:

1. Whatever

2. Could be

3. I have not thought of that

4. You might be right

5. Hmmm maybe I am

6. You are right

7. You are the expert

8. I don't care\so what

9. Thanks for sharing that

10. I like being…thanks

11. When did you start feeling this\that way

12. I did not know you felt this way

13. Thanks-see ya

It is important to understand that young people who are in the situation of being inappropriately teased do not want to use these words to escalate the situation. Instead, teach them to use these phrases as they begin to walk away from the person who is inappropriately teasing them.

Many times I will hear from students that some of the most popular kids in a school are the same kids who bully others. Some people think that kids (or for that matter adults) who bully have low self-esteem, and that may be true for some. However, many who bully have an inflated ego. They have a destructive appetite for power and control. The ability to stop the bullying behavior in a school or community comes from bystanders who represent the majority of the student body. There is power in numbers. Besides telling an adult that someone is being bullied, there are several strategies bystanders can use to help support those being bullied:

- *Distract the bully.* If you are with a friend who begins to tease someone else, quickly distract your friend by changing the subject or asking him a question. You would be keeping your friend out of trouble, but, more importantly, helping the person who is being teased or bullied.

- *Support the person who is being bullied privately.* If you could not get the person or persons to stop the bullying behavior, for whatever reason, go back to the person who was being bullied and support them privately. You could say *"I am sorry for what my friend said, or those other kids said, and I will talk to them about it to see if I can get the bullying behavior to stop."*

- *Support the person who is being bullied openly.* I only recommend this strategy to kids who feel confident and have a certain amount of respect among their peers.

- *Do not feed into the bully behavior.* Don't laugh at their jokes if they are humiliating someone, and do not promote or attend a fight. As bystanders, it is your responsibility to de-escalate the situation, not feed fuel to an already hot fire.

If you have a child or teenager being bullied, please contact your school counselor and set up an appointment to discuss the situation. The administration and other adults may need to get involved in making sure the bullying behavior stops. The biggest issue in getting help for the child or teenager who is into bullying behavior often is breaking through the parent's denial that their child or teen may be a bully. It is important that we identify and label the behavior as bullying behavior. The chances of being successful with intervention strategies are great, especially when the behavior can be identified at an early age.

One Particular Class

I was doing work with a 5th-grade class on getting along with each other, when a little boy started to cry. He was about 30 pounds overweight and wore his hair down in his eyes and gently began to rise out of his seat. This is what he shared with the class: "*I'm fat and I know people stare at me, they stare at my parents when we go out to eat. It is hard for me to lose weight. I thought school would be a place where kids wouldn't pick on me. I just wish you could look past my weight and give me a chance.*" The class response was mixed. Some kids laughed, some cried. The teacher was crying. I went on and explained the difference to the class between teasing and bullying behavior.

I had them take out a piece of paper and asked them to think of kids in their class who they would consider fit the description of a bully and write those names down. Immediately two kids put their heads down while another raised his hand and asked what I was going to do with the names. I told them that if their name appeared more than three times I would meet with those kids with the expectation that the bullying behavior would stop. If it did not stop, their parents would be called. The child who raised his hand to ask the question did not think that was fair. My response was simple. "*What is not fair is a kid not being allowed to attend school without being called names, put down, and shamed in front of their friends. If you are not following the teasing rules and have crossed over into bullying behavior, it needs to stop. There are adults who can help you with this if you are open to help.*" Those three boys' names appeared on 18 out of 24 lists. They were in fact making one young 5th grader's life miserable.

When I speak to high school kids about bullying, I speak about how people choose to use their gifts. I explain to them that they all have certain gifts: some people are excellent listeners, others are organized, and some have academic gifts, while others may know a trade. I explain that if one gift of theirs is sports or strength and they choose to use it by putting others down, I have no respect for them. They should all use their gifts to help encourage and support each other.

I hear from kids that boys or girls who do not fit into the boxes that kids like to place each other in (and adults for that matter) automatically can become targets to a certain extent. Boys who do not like sports, or do not have sports ability, are sometimes labeled "gay," especially if they enjoy drama, art and non-traditional hobbies and activities that many boys don't. Non-traditional girls can be treated the same way. I also want you to remember that bullying is not just a kid thing. Some parents, other adults and even some teachers and administrators bully. Why won't kids help the child who is being bullied?

- They do not have a clear understanding of bullying.

- They confuse teasing with bullying.

- They think that boys will be boys and girls will be girls.

- The bully might turn on them.

- They want to be popular.

- They have a lack of empathy.

- They do not want to get involved.

- They have a lack of support.

- They do not know what to do.

- There is no safe way to report bullying.

- They may lose friends.

- If the kid who is being picked on hangs out with perceived "losers," the bystander may be afraid to support him or her for fear of affiliation.

Remember that girls bully as well as boys, but they tend to use different behaviors. Girls are likely to spread rumors, ostracize people—and a best friend on Friday may be the enemy on Monday. When they bully, boys tend to use physical and verbal insults, intimidation or threats. (If you'd like to learn more about girls and bullying, check out *Odd Girl Out* by Rachel Simmons or *Girl Wars* by Cheryl Dellasega, Ph.D. and Charisse Nixon, Ph.D.)

If Your Child is Bullied

Here are some things to do if your child is being bullied:

• Report bullying behavior to the school.

• Report bullying behavior to the police if necessary.

• Involve your school counselor, administrator, and your child's teachers. Find out as much information as you can.

• Be a detective; document everything.

• Take pictures of torn clothes, books, and bruises if there is physical bullying present.

• Remember, the goal here is to see that the bullying behavior ends.

• Sometimes peer mediation can work, if it is early in the bully/target cycle, and both parties agree. Parents can get the kids together if the relationship between the bully and the target has not progressed to physical violence, threats, or intimidation.

There are exceptions to these rules. Many times kids come home and tell their parents that they are being bullied, but do not want you to call the school for fear of retribution because they might get kids in trouble, or they feel shamed or embarrassed, or they worry that it'll just make things worse. Talk to your child about both of you finding an adult at the school to brainstorm with, someone that you trust. The school counselor is a good place to start.

If your child is not in immediate danger, then you have some flexibility; however, if there are safety concerns or your child is in immediate danger, then you must report the behavior immediately. I have known families who have had to make a geographic move for the bullying behavior to stop. It is important to note that if your child is bringing some of this bullying behavior onto themselves through their own actions, then a move may help, but the bullying behavior may begin once again. Many kids are picked on for no reason at all; others are picked on because they bring some of it on themselves. This could be due to lack of social skills or other reasons. This child is called a provocative victim as defined by Dan Olweus in his book *Bullying At School* (In either case, we must get the bullying behavior to stop first before we can address the issue). Some strategies that may work with the kids who are being bullied include, but are not limited to: assertiveness training, social skills group, self-defense classes, and outside counseling. If your child is being picked on and is doing nothing to bring that behavior on, which happens in many cases, once the bullying behavior stops, no other strategy may be needed. Please keep in mind that the bully may also benefit from social skills groups along with some outside counseling. Each situation for both the bully and the child who is being bullied must be evaluated and the parents must be willing to be open to the strategies that are suggested. **(See Appendix E for ways on talking to your child if they report being bullied or you receive a call from the school or another parent stating your child is exhibiting bullying behavior).**

Many kids tease and pick on others by using e-mail, instant messaging, and chat rooms. It is much more impersonal and many times kids can say things over e-mail and in chat rooms that they would not say in person. (**See Appendix F for an article on cyber bullying by Dr. Patti Agatston**)

Most of my research suggests that somewhere between 40 to 60 percent of kids are teased, which coincides with other research, but most of those kids have enough support systems in place to weather the storm. In any given school when kids are asked the question, "*Have you ever stayed home from school and played sick because you were being picked on or teased,*" about three to eight percent would respond yes. That would be around 30 to 80 young people for every 1000, and frankly, I would have been counted among those when I was in school. Would you have? Please talk to your kids about teasing and bullying.

Before we move on, I want to make a quick comment about zero tolerance policies and their relation to bullying and threats of violence. There is a difference between a student who is exhibiting bullying behavior through their words and is threatening another student, as opposed to a student who is a target of bullying behavior and makes a threatening comment because they are at their wits end and have not been successful at getting the bullying behavior to stop. I agree, both students are in the wrong for making a threatening comment, but do you see the need for some flexibility here? Most zero tolerance policies carry with them minimum days out of school for first and second offenses. It would be more logical to have a policy that states a student can be suspended for up to five days for the first offense and allow the administration to decide where within that policy each individual case would fall. Do we need consistent policies? Yes we do, but please let's give our administrators some flexibility in how they implement and enforce those policies.

Post-September 11th

I remember a song called "Dear God" by XTC that starts off with a little girl asking God questions about why we have so many problems here on earth and whether God has forsaken us. The song questions the foundation that many religions are based on and debates the question as to why humans justify fighting in the name of God. This song came to mind when I was meeting with several young people after delivering a drug talk. I was trying to find out what some of their thoughts were in regards to going to middle school. As one way of keeping up with youth trends, thoughts and issues that they face, I like to meet with kids randomly chosen by their teachers. I asked them what some of their fears were of attending middle school the next year. Here is what they had to say:

- Being asked to do drugs

- Homework

- Parents' expectations

- Being picked on by 8th graders

- Changing in the locker-room

- Getting lost

- Not being able to open their locker

- Not having any friends

Most 10-year-olds would come up with this list of common fears. Gangs would be an issue also for those who live in communities where gang activity exists. I asked these kids if there were any other fears they had that they'd like to share with the group. One little girl raised her hand and mentioned anthrax. I asked her where she heard about anthrax, and she cited the news. Another little girl raised her hand and said, "*I am worried about war.*" A little boy raised his hand and said that he was told by his mother not to share with other kids that he was Jewish for safety reasons. The kids looked at each other somewhat perplexed by the little boy's response. *"I'm this religion,"* responded one child, while another said *"I am a Christian,"* and still another said, *"Are not those two things the same?"* We then got into a discussion about school prayer. I asked the kids these questions: *"What if all of the schools had school prayer? What do you think that would look like?"* Here is what they had to say.

"Somebody would come into the school and lead everyone in a prayer. We would all be asked to sit with kids who shared the same religion we did. And we would not like that. What happens to those kids who don't have anybody to sit next to because nobody in the class believes like they do? What happens if we all begin to pray and one person gets sad because that is not how their parents taught them to pray?" One student suggested that they already pray before they hand in their homework—they hope for a good grade. I think most of us can relate to that! Kids can be pretty amazing. They can sit down at a table and talk about issues openly without agendas, without politics, and get right to the issue at hand. This was no ordinary group because it took place several weeks after September 11th. They had a lot on their minds. Their perception of what school prayer might look like may seem somewhat distorted to you, but the truth may lie somewhere in the middle. I have been to many public conferences and school PTA meetings where someone leads the group into prayer before the meeting starts. Usually the prayer is Christian-based, with no intent to disrespect others who may not believe in the Christian faith. However, when people are asked to bow their heads in public prayer, do you think the prayer should be more generic in nature, knowing that not everyone in the audience believes in what the person leading the prayer suggests? Would you be offended if someone led you in prayer that contradicted your beliefs? Should religious prayer specific to one or two faiths be said at school, public meetings or conferences? Is it ever possible to make all faiths feel comfortable within the realm of public organized prayer?

Mixing it up: Diversity and Tolerance

There is a song by Everclear called "Heartspark Dollarsign" that talks about interracial dating. I have talked to kids about this song before and asked them if interracial dating is an issue for them. Most say it is not, but that it is for most of their parents. This will come up during high school trainings, along with diversity issues in general. There has been much written on the subject of diversity, and I still get calls about how kids are sitting in the cafeteria. Why aren't they mixing? My response is: Is their failure to mix creating problems for the school or for the students at large? If black students want to sit with one another during lunch, what is wrong with that? What is wrong with sitting next to someone who you share a connection with, especially if the majority of students in the school are white? It becomes a big deal, however, if kids won't *allow* others to sit with them because of race, faith, or popularity. If that happens, it needs to be addressed immediately. If you are going to promote diversity, it is important to go deeper than black, white, Latino, Asian, and so on. In an earlier chapter, I talked about cliques and the perceived differences between the groups of kids that exist in every school. Once we begin to label one another, it becomes more difficult to sit down at the table and talk.

I use the following chart with high school kids, to illustrate how quickly we move from the initial labeling of the person to the aggressive act that can take place when there is conflict.

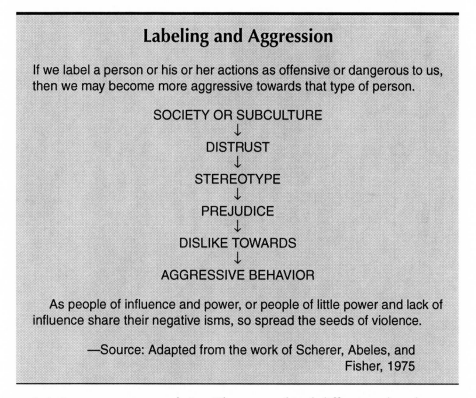

Labeling and Aggression

If we label a person or his or her actions as offensive or dangerous to us, then we may become more aggressive towards that type of person.

SOCIETY OR SUBCULTURE
↓
DISTRUST
↓
STEREOTYPE
↓
PREJUDICE
↓
DISLIKE TOWARDS
↓
AGGRESSIVE BEHAVIOR

As people of influence and power, or people of little power and lack of influence share their negative isms, so spread the seeds of violence.

—Source: Adapted from the work of Scherer, Abeles, and Fisher, 1975

It is important not to polarize. There are cultural differences, but there are probably more differences *within* races than *between* them. Trying to connect kids and give them a sense of belonging—no matter who they are, what they believe in, or what they look like—while acknowledging and celebrating the cultural differences among us is what diversity is all about.

26

Angry Kids

Parents, do you know any angry kids? Let me begin by asking you some questions:

- How did you handle your anger while growing up?

- How did other people in your house express their anger?

- How do you handle your anger now?

I know you have heard this before, but anger in itself can be healthy. Most of the civil rights movement used anger as a catalyst for change. Nonsmokers who were tired of breathing in someone else's smoke changed a norm that most people thought could never be changed. Whether you agree with those changes or not, it is incredible what people can accomplish when anger is channeled in the right direction.

I have worked with many kids over the years who were very angry about a variety of things that have happened to them in their lives. I also receive many calls from parents who are concerned about their child being very angry. I've noticed that most angry kids I have worked with in the past seem to listen to similar kinds of music and I've always been curious about the gravitational pull toward aggressive genres of music. I am not suggesting that only angry kids listen to those types of music, but I did want to ask the question. Here is what I've heard from kids about why they listen to aggressive music:

- *"I like the drive and the insane feeling that it brings on in me."*

- *"I like how aggressive music calms me down."*

- *"I like the words 'f**k you.'"*

- *"Power, lots of power."*

- *"I like how rap and metal challenge authority."*

- *"It gives me a sense of hope."*

- *"'80s metal had some sense you could take on the world and win. '90s metal said you can take on the world and kick its ass."*

- *"I get to live vicariously through the music."*

- *"Girls, sex, cars, and drugs—what else is there?"*

- *"Get out of my way, motherf**ker. You don't want to mess with me."*

- *"I just like how it sounds."*

- *"It helps me get out my energy and calms me down. I'm ADHD."*

- *"When I am pissed off, the music agrees with how I am feeling."*

Metal went away for a while, but is now attracting a much wider audience due to in part the crossover in comics and movies. Movies like *The One* and *xXx* have metal soundtracks. Kids who may not normally listen to metal have been introduced to the genre through other mediums. The same can be said for rap.

It is important to understand that many kids have pretty good reasons for being angry. I got a call the other day from a dad whose 7th grade son was getting into fights with other students. The father couldn't understand why his son was fighting, so I began to ask if anything was going on in the family, and how long he has seen this kind of behavior being exhibited by his son. He told me that he was recently divorced and his ex-wife was about to remarry. I'm not excusing his son's behavior, but in this context, it is easy to understand the boy's anger. Kids are resilient, in many cases more resilient than we are, but they grieve too, and they need time to adjust to a situation and process it, just like we do. Sometimes the choices they make during this grieving process need our attention. Sometimes they need more than schools can provide.

There are those students who don't just get angry from time to time, but who use their anger in destructive ways. Maybe it has to do with temperament issues, modeling behavior, or other factors that exist in a child's life.

Kids who have a history of chronic anger I sometimes compare to kids who are addicted to drugs. Some kids, when angry, feel a sense of euphoria or a quick rush. Others feel a complete loss of control or an overwhelming sense of powerlessness over their anger. They cannot control it once they release it. Others take no responsibility for their anger and believe that their problem with expressing it inappropriately is due to others provoking them. Many of these kids become enmeshed in a culture of music that validates who they are and how they feel. To some extent, the music rationalizes their behaviors in their own minds. For some, it allows them to express themselves through their music as opposed to hurting others or themselves. (For more information on working with angry and hostile kids, check out *The Explosive Child* by Ross Greene, Ph.D.)

Most elementary school teachers and counselors will tell you that they can identify students by the 3rd grade, who without an intervention, may go on to develop emotional and academic problems. This is the reason so many prevention strategies begin during elementary school. Violence prevention and life skills programs—that introduce student to concepts like problem solving, empathy, anger management skills, and refusal skills—are being offered in schools across the country. Conflict Resolution, peace tables, youth leadership, and peer mediation programs are also being used in the schools to encourage kids to talk out their problems, as opposed to getting into fights over "he said/she said" kinds of issues.

There are kids who are depressed, using drugs, angry and hostile, and others that are dealing with a multitude of issues in their lives who need much more than the school can offer. For those youth, a complete evaluation needs to be conducted before strategies can be put in place. The type of treatment or response depends on the length of time they have been expressing themselves in this way, severity of the problem, frequency of the problem, and other factors that need to be evaluated. Emotions Anonymous, another twelve-step program like Alcoholics Anonymous and Narcotics Anonymous, encourages youth and adults to look at how their emotions are out of control.

Some youth may need counseling with someone experienced in working with angry and hostile kids. Some of these kids are clinically depressed, others undiagnosed, and some may even need to be hospitalized. Use your school as a resource. Talk with the school counselor, school social worker and psychologist, along with your child's teachers and administrators, to formulate a plan of action. We must all work together if we are going to make a difference in a child's life. What usually gets in the way of working together is a lack of trust; we must overcome this lack of trust if we are going to be successful in raising healthy drug-free kids.

Depression

Have you ever felt this way?
Always feeling out of place
Hiding behind a smiling face
There just ain't no pretty words
*"Can't you see it f****n' hurts!*
*You know I feel like s**t—déjà vu*
*Feel like s**t—déjà vu"*

"S**T—DÉJÀ VU"
(lyrics by Mike Muir and Rocky George)
Suicidal Tendencies

Many kids I have worked with have expressed feeling this way. It is important to recognize that some kids who appear angry on the surface may really be depressed.

- Do you see depression as something a person just snaps out of?

- Is there depression in your family?

- Do you believe teenagers or children can be clinically depressed?

- Why do you think we do not have more men being diagnosed with depression? Could it be that men and boys have a tendency to drink, or use other drugs, to deal with their depression as opposed to many women who talk about their problems instead?

- Do you look at depression as a sign of weakness?

- Have you ever been depressed—not clinically depressed, just sad or down—and you find sad music to put on and listen to or watch a sad movie? Does it make you feel better?

Why is it that so many kids are being diagnosed with depression and other disorders:

- *Knowledge.* We know more than we ever have. When you were growing up did you have any friends on medication for depression, ADHD, bipolar disorder, or other disorders?

- *Change in community and family structure.* We are much more mobile than we have been in the past, which contributes to a breakdown in the community and family structure.

- *Fewer interpersonal relationships.* Relationships have changed, often as a result of technology that links and connects people "virtually."

- *Academic pressure.* Kids truly learn differently, and expectations of young people are changing. I really don't know if I started school all over again today if I would make it through academically. Do you think you would? Better yet, do you think you would get the same grades that you did when you were in school?

- *Adult trends.* Many children model parents' mood, style, and habits. It is challenging enough to be a parent, let alone a parent who is depressed and is not receiving the support they need.

- *Insurance.* If in counseling, a child must be presented with a diagnosis in order for insurance to cover the costs.

Symptoms of Depression

- *A sense of hopelessness.* In working with suicidal youth, I have found that a sense of hopelessness is a factor in kids attempting suicide. Sometimes this may look like powerlessness or a sense of no control over one's life. Simply put, these kids see no light at the end of the tunnel.

- *Mood.* You may notice that your child has exaggerated mood swings; sad, low or flat affect; irritability; is easily frustrated; is crying a lot, or can't cry. Sometimes in very young children you may see some regressive behavior, especially if the child just experienced a loss. Older kids and teens may become aggressive or belligerent toward people they love.

- *Interest.* Loss of friends, hobbies, school in general.

- *Changes.* In friends, music, clothes, sleep, food, exercise, weight.

- *Agitated and restless or sluggish* (seen more in adults). Many adults and teens will use alcohol or other drugs during this time.

- *Overall loss of energy*

- *Worthlessness, shame, and/or guilt.* Many kids who are being bullied feel they cannot protect themselves, and much of the bullying happens in front of their peers, which can become a shame-based experience.

- *Impaired concentration and focus*

- *Anxiety, panic attacks, worry, obsessions, somatic complaints*

- *Cutting.* There may be other forms of self-mutilation, as well as cutting on self, but cutters are not generally suicidal. (See Appendix G)

- *Suicidal Ideation.* A child having thoughts or a plan of suicide may require taking the child for an assessment; although each situation may require different intervention strategies.

- *Increasingly hostile.* Sadness can turn to rage.

Many of these symptoms can be signs of other types of illnesses such as anxiety disorders, bipolar disorder, etc. Length of time, frequency, cluster of symptoms, and severity of the symptoms all come into play when diagnosing depression.

—Source: Adapted from *Cognitive: Behavioral Treatment of Depression*, Klosko and Sanderso

Suicidal Ideation

A few years ago, I received a call from a father who just lost his son to suicide. His son was into a genre of music that represented hopelessness and despair. He asked me if I would support him in trying to change the legislation in his community to

make purchasing certain kinds of music illegal until the age of 21. He acknowl-
edged that there were many factors involved that led to his son's suicide, but felt
strongly that the music his son was listening to was having a negative influence on
him and may have contributed to his son taking his own life. The father was not
aware of what his son was listening to until after the suicide took place. This
raises the question about the power music may have on some individuals and the
potential for music to be abused by listeners. The bands in question, of course,
are protected by the First Amendment, but this is a tragic tale that has repeated
itself time and time again. From Ozzy Osborne to Judas Priest, bands have been
sued because parents have felt strongly that certain lyrics can have a negative
impact on kids and that musicians have a responsibly to their listeners. It is
important to understand that, for some kids, music suggests a lifestyle, values,
norms, and an overall culture that can lead an already depressed child into
despair. It can also lead that same child out of despair by validating how he feels,
becoming his only friend. Therein lies the debate. The following are strategies for
parents to consider if suicidal ideation is a concern:

- *Know your child; look for changes.* Pay attention to behaviors that are not within
  the norm of your child's peer group or other kids the same age. (A counselor
  can help with this.) The most important thing you can do is *listen* to what
  your child is saying and look for those things that go unsaid. See if your child
  is keeping to himself more, or check to see if he has been giving possessions
  away. Check in with your child's friends once in a while. Talk to him every-
  day. Even if he does not talk back, he hears you.

- *Find out if they are suicidal.* If you have an adult friend who appears depressed,
  or your child appears depressed to you, ask the question, "*Have you thought
  about killing yourself?*" or say, "*I know you must be going through a very hard
  time right now—are you thinking about hurting yourself?*" This will not put
  thoughts of suicide in their heads. I am asked that question all the time by parents with a child who appears depressed or who has made some comment
  about hurting himself. Many parents whose child has lost a friend to suicide
  worry that their child might do the same thing, whether they talk about it or
  not. Is that a possibility? Yes, it is, but it is highly unlikely, unless the child
  already had the thoughts in his head or has several issues going on in his life at
  the time of the suicide. It is important to ask the question. If you feel uncomfortable asking the question, find someone who will.

- *If someone will not go for help alone, offer to go along.* If the person still refuses to
  get help, see if she would be willing to agree not to harm herself until a new

strategy can be put in place. If it is your child who is thinking about suicide, you have much more control over getting her some help, whether she wants it or not. I believe prevention strategies can and do work when it comes to preventing suicide. If parents and educators are knowledgeable about the risks, warning signs, and language to use with those who may be in a crisis, it can help lower the odds of completed suicides.

I do know there are young people and adults who, even after interventions are put in place, still take their own lives. No matter how many roadblocks are put in place, some things are out of our control. But we must continue to be vigilant. All of us are responsible for doing prevention. The most difficult part of my job is walking into a school and spending the day with adults and young people who are grieving the loss of a family member or friend. Every crisis is different and every crisis reminds us just how precious life really is. (From a young person's point of view, check out the book, *Conquering the Beast Within*, by Cait Irwin). There is a song I am reminded of when I am talking to kids who may be depressed, sad, or just wanting to get away:

"Everybody hurts
Take comfort in your friends
Everybody hurts
Don't throw your hand. Oh, no
Don't throw your hand
If you feel like you're alone
No, no, no, you are not alone"

"Everybody Hurts"
R.E.M.
(To learn more about child and adolescent depression, check out *Help Me I'm Sad* by David G. Fassler and Lynne Dumas.)

27

For Educators and Parents

"Hey teacher, leave those kids alone!"

Pink Floyd

There are so many examples of educators helping kids through very difficult times that will never be captured on any evaluation form or written into anyone's job description. Maybe that is what "no child left behind" really means.

Why is there a chapter for educators in a self-help book for parents? As I stated in the introduction, I believe it is important to have this conversation with parents and educators alike. The relationship that parents and educators develop with each other impacts our kids. In 20-plus years of working with youth, I have never found them to be so academically stressed as they are today. As kids are becoming more stressed, so are the educators that work with them—for a variety of reasons. At the same time, parents have become critical of the educational system as a whole and, although most educators do walk in parents' shoes, most parents have never been educators. I am trying to get parents and educators to understand each other's perspectives because our behavior impacts kids. It is about the kids, isn't it?

I would like to begin with a dream I had…

The Dream

(Why is it everyone thinks they can teach)?

It is approaching the end of another school year—or is it the beginning—where I find myself presenting to thousands of people on the responsibilities of being a teacher...

Understand that you have some students who are: ODD, OC, ADHD, EBD, BD, LFT, Gifted (they are all gifted), some who speak limited English or no English at all, kids who use ATOD, kids who are undiagnosed, and kids who just kind of get by.
Which means you really need to familiarize yourself in the following topic areas:

Right Brain Thinking, Whole Brain Thinking, Positive Discipline, Cultural Diversity, Anxiety Disorders, Phobias, Pharmacology, Eating Disorders, Communication Skills, Verbal Self Defense, Family Counseling, Interior Design, Take Down Techniques, Drama, Time Management, Mediation, Technology,
Conflict Resolution, Bully Prevention, Physical, Sexual, and Emotional Abuse, Violence Prevention, Personal Safety Issues, Suicidal and Homicidal Ideation, Portfolio Building, Grief and Loss Work, Gangs, Stress and Anger Management, Behavior Mod, Cognitive Therapy, Rational Emotive Therapy,
Reality Therapy, Peer Programs, Political Correctness, Leadership Training, Public Speaking, Active Listening, Crisis Response, School Law and Policies, and being **effective as well as entertaining in the classroom.**

You must learn to go the bathroom during planning, lunch or scheduled bathroom breaks. (You might want to bring your own toilet paper as the one that is provided can cause extreme pain.).

You must have lesson plans made in advance that must fit into the curriculum objectives that must coincide with the QCCs. Am I saying the same thing twice? Repeating yourself will become a common occurrence.

You must monitor students at all times. When they are in the: hall, bathroom, cafeteria (teachers are allowed to socialize and enjoy a 15–30 minute lunch break each and every day), recess (if recess is permitted at your school), and all drills and field trips.

You will be required to attend all scheduled faculty meetings, workshops, staff development, PTA, and committee meetings as needed.

You will be responsible for teaching the curriculum while establishing and maintaining control of all the students in your class along with their parents' support. In order to communicate effectively with parents you may be instructed to use e-mail, phone calls, newsletters, report cards, conferences, and IEP meetings.

You will be expected to create a **friendly classroom climate** to include posters, books, supplies, shelves, rewards, food, stickers, music, color schemes, extra lighting, and supplemental guides. Some of the money for these supplies will be budgeted.
The rest will need to come from you.
Higher education is encouraged—the money to pay for it comes from you. Try working part time during your summers off.

You may use the one copier that works to run off needed materials. Please be patient.

Please learn the phrase "Think outside the box."
If you are used to being assertive—please stop. Your opinion is no longer needed.
Retirement awaits you.

Understand that many evenings and weekends will be spent grading papers and preparing you for the next day. This is a 24\7 job.

Please remember—every day must be a good day. You will not be allowed to show feelings that may be associated with having a bad day.

Remember, you will be evaluated on how well students do on their standardized tests.
That is the bottom line. Please remind parents not to compare test results in front of their children. (My child scored higher in math than yours). Please advise the students to drink plenty of water, eat a good breakfast, and get plenty of rest. Have a great day, and remember that all students come ready to learn.

As I gather my belongings and make a mad dash for the door, the bell is ringing and I realize my alarm is going off. It was all a dream.

> **A dream. Smiling, as I begin to take on a new day, I realize how amazing I am. Not every one can do what I do. I am truly gifted!**

Is there any truth to this poem? I decided to write it for two reasons. One was that I know how hard educators work, and I also know they are not respected like they once were. The other reason I wrote this poem was that I substituted once for a 3rd grade class. No, everybody is not a teacher, but most people think they can teach.

Adults today have become experts at everything. We can learn about any subject now that we have access to the information through the Internet and other resources. Forty years ago, we never would have questioned our doctors, but now we see prescription drugs advertised on television and we've become experts on which drugs are best for us to take. We have hundreds of medical and psychological Web sites we can turn to for help in self-diagnosing the problem. When we go to doctors, many of us feel we know more than they do about what the problem is and how to treat it.

The once-powerful medical model is now questioned by consumers who use herbs and alternative healing methods to address diseases that alternative providers claim they can cure. This is coupled with apathy over insurance and HMOs that consumers feel care more about the money (very few seem to cover any kind of wellness or preventative care) than they do about the patient. The wealth of information available today has allowed consumers to challenge professions that were once unchallengeable and off-limits. Doctors are caught in the middle, and consumers just aren't sure whom to believe anymore. Education is no different. Parents seem to be challenging school policies, teaching methods, school boards, superintendents and principals because they have been told that the only way to measure success is through high test scores.

Who sold us the notion that high test scores equal success? When I sat down years ago to take the ITBS in elementary school, I had no clue what it was and how it was going to be used. Standardized tests used to be a tool for helping the teacher identify areas that a particular student needed to focus on and then sharing that area of focus with the parents. How has that changed? I now have parents who compare their child's test scores to their neighbor's child's test scores. Sometimes they do this in front of their kids. There are newspapers that sell out the day the test scores are released, so parents can compare their school's scores to those of other schools. I know teachers who spend hours using the scores to calculate the growth of their students. Should a teacher's only measure of success be based on test scores? Should your child's only measure of success be based on the scores he receives?

I was looking for a pre-school for my son several years ago. I called one particular private school and this is what they had to say, "*We will teach your child addition and subtraction, along with a healthy dose of science, and we will begin to plant those academic seeds. I know you are concerned about test scores, so let me assure you that our test scores are higher than most public schools' test scores.*" I interrupted her to ask if my child would be introduced to art and be allowed to draw, sing songs, play, and learn how to get along with others in a small-group setting. He was three or four years old at the time. This particular school had a waiting list for enrollment.

When some elementary schools across this country must cut recess to meet curriculum needs, you have to ask yourself if we have gone too far. What is next? Eliminating health and physical education, art and music? I realize that educators must be held accountable and must be responsible to the community at large, and I know that measuring test scores is one way to do that, but let's see if we can work together to bring some balance back to the field of education. Why talk about this topic here in a prevention book, because parents and educators need to have this conversation and learn to work *with* each other, not *against* each other.

Isn't it amazing to think that every day a school bell rings, and thousands of kids in any one particular school get to where they are supposed to be? Each and every day, it is the principal's responsibility, along with the rest of the faculty, to enforce the rules to the best of their abilities, rules that many people in the community find punitive and at times illogical. Yet, I wonder if all families had a dress code, zero tolerance towards drug use, violence, and bullying behavior, if we would not find ourselves treating each other with a little bit more respect and compassion. Then maybe music, television, movies, and print would begin to reflect a different image of who we are and who we are trying to be.

The community wants high academic standards while expecting safe schools. Who doesn't want that? But how we reach our goal is up for much debate. When I started doing prevention work, I could pull students from classes two to three days to train in peer mediation. Today, that training is down to a half-day or a day at the most. I can't get the kids out of class because of academic restraints. Educators and parents alike need to be able to draw the connection between academic performance and social skills. So, whose responsibility is it to teach those social skills?

Many parents say they will provide social skills to their children and that schools should only be responsible for academics, but what about those parents who are not providing these skills to their kids? If the community at large is having problems with gangs, drugs or any number of social issues that impact kids today, many parents in the community expect the school to have programs and or strategies in place to address them. Who in the school should be responsible for implementing such strategies? Should the school counselor be responsible for implementing all of these programs?

Most counselors will tell you that they would love to do support groups, research-based programs, and strategies that would address some of those social issues we are talking about, and many are. In order for high school counselors to do these things, they would have to stop doing the filing and the testing and the registering of students. When you take into account the fact that they are also responsible for advisement and helping students with college admission needs, having to carry a caseload of 300 to 500 students at a time, it becomes an issue of practicality. How do you prioritize all of those things, when you really can't leave out any of them because you are responsible for all of them? How can we expect the school to be safe when the same kids who help make the community unsafe go to that school?

We have parents who get upset when they find out there may be kids smoking pot in the school bathroom—they want the school to address it, and the school needs to do so. But some of these same parents who are calling the school with their concerns are also providing alcohol to their kids and their kid's friends on a Saturday night. Here are some thoughts on qualities both parents and educators should foster in order to improve the relationship between the two sectors:

- *Direct communication.* If you or your child has a problem with a teacher, make an appointment to talk about the issue. At that meeting, ask the teacher if it would be helpful to schedule another conference with the child present (depending on the age of the child and situation). If you are not satisfied with the outcome of the conference, you could follow it up with a request to meet with an administrator. If that does not work, you can request to talk with the principal or the principal's supervisor. Please understand that some of the most difficult and demanding parents are those who work in the field of education. We all want what's best for our kids. I challenge you to look back into your own childhood or the teachers that your own children are growing up with now, and you will probably find more teachers who were caring, concerned, and made an attempt to connect with you or your child than those who were critical, negative and closed-minded.

- *Tolerance.* Educators shouldn't be so quick to judge parents of an unruly child. Sometimes parents don't know what to do with the child either. Sometimes the educator doesn't know what strategies the parent has tried in hopes of helping their child.

- *Collaboration.* If you have a child in therapy, please consider having a two way communication release form signed so somebody at the school can be included in the treatment plan.

- *Character education.* Make sure character education begins at home.

- *Acceptance.* Do not judge a school by one walk through. You would not want your home to be judged by one unannounced walk through.

- *Information.* Parents, please go over the rules in the school handbook with your child at the beginning, middle, and right before the end of the school year.

- *Responsibility.* Sometimes educators complain about parents having their heads in the sand when it comes to drug use in a particular community and, in many cases, they are correct. But the same can be said for some educators, who feel that drug use isn't happening in their schools, and try to make it solely a community issue. The problem belongs to all of us. We need each other to address it.

- *Professionalism.* Educators must treat each other as professionals regardless of the positions that each person holds in that particular school. Educators must also advocate for themselves to feel a sense of empowerment and control over their profession.

- *Education.* Parents need to learn more about the roles that different educators play in a school. Most parents do not understand what the role of a school counselor, psychologist, or social worker is. It is our job to educate the community. It is the parent's job to ask the question if they do not know.

- *Feedback.* If you invite parents in for feedback, then listen to what they have to say. Teachers, if you welcome feedback from your parents only when it is positive, then no growth can take place. Sometimes schools want parental involvement as long as that involvement doesn't rock the boat. At the same time, there are schools being run by three or four powerful parents in the community who have the school and its principal constantly under its watchful eye, mistaking the public school for a private school. There are also situations where schools internally have conflict due to an imbalance of power within the school. If something is wrong, then talk about it and address it. Isn't that what we try to teach our kids?

- *Perspective.* Do not judge a school by the data it collects. When you look at discipline numbers, understand that 90 percent of the infractions may be caused by 5 to 10 percent of the student body.

- *Awareness.* Many schools across the country will not participate in violence or drug surveys because they do not want the numbers getting out into the community, for fear that the school may be labeled. The community doesn't want to do the surveys either, for fear that the school might be labeled violent or "druggie" and their property values might decrease as people move out. I have heard this for the last 14 years I have been a prevention specialist. One cannot begin to address the issues unless both parties agree to it. We cannot solve a problem without identifying the question.

- *Service.* Parents can get to know their child's school by volunteering their services.

- *Intergenerational learning.* I always thought senior squads would be a good idea. I envision this as a group of grandmas and grandpas who walk the halls to keep the peace. Sometimes kids act a little different around senior citizens. Plus, many kids who do not relate well to their peers relate well to older adults. I think many seniors would enjoy being in a position of mentorship, a natural role for the senior squad to take.

- *Relationships.* The more open and honest we are with each other without fear of retribution, the greater the impact we will have on our kids and community at large.

For more information addressing prevention strategies for schools, please see the Prevention Plan in Appendix C.

28

Neighborhoods and Communities

I will have parents approach me after a workshop and say, "*Don't you think kids were better-behaved in the 50s?*" Life just seemed more innocent then; people treated each other with more respect. What would your response to that question be? My response would be "*It would depend on what side of the tracks you lived on.*"

What kind of community did you grow up in? I remember the song "Ball of Confusion" by the Temptations. I believe the song's lyrics have stood the test of time. The song talks about issues that most of us today still struggle with: drug use, white flight and changing neighborhoods, gun control, taxes, fear, suicide, and revolution. I can remember singing it out loud, but I didn't really internalize the words. I encourage all of you to listen to that song one more time.

What kind of neighborhood did you grow up in? Was it safe? Did you leave your door open at night? Twenty years ago I drove a young man home; we had just terminated him from treatment. Back in the old days of drug treatment, the strategies and techniques were a little bit different from today. "Termination" was a word used when the adolescent did everything he could do to force the staff's hand and was asked to leave treatment. The adolescent's clothes would be taken and put in the middle of a large circle where all of his peers would be waiting to give him feedback and say goodbye.

No matter what the feedback was, the person in the middle could not respond. After the circle activity was completed, either the parents would come to pick up their child or a staff member would drive him home. When this particular young man got in the car and told me the directions to his home, I soon realized where he lived. His house was in an area loaded with gang graffiti, abandoned homes that were boarded up, and there was an alleged crack house across the street. When his mother came to the door, she had alcohol on her breath. She thanked me for driving him home and then she disappeared into another room.

The young man and I talked for about an hour and then it was time for me to go. One of the questions he asked me while we were talking was, *"Have you ever gone to bed knowing that you might be awakened by a gunshot? I hear those once in a while, while I'm trying to sleep."* His world—his life and his perspective—was entirely different from mine. What that young man taught me was something I carry with me today. He made no excuses for his behavior. He knew he had messed up. He knew he had been given the opportunity to change his life, but he just wasn't there yet. He was surviving. He lived in a place that he called "home," and it was a place most of us would not even want to pass through. How much we learn about these kids when we are given the chance to see where they live, who they live with, and how they live. But do you think that is only true for the neighborhood I just described?

It is easy to go into any inner city area and take pictures of a drug deal going down or see a prostitute walking the street. It is easy to watch a television show that depicts a low-income neighborhood riddled with gang activity, drug use, and violence. It is much more difficult to visualize young Johnny knocking on the door of a $300,000 home, being greeted by fifteen-year-old Suzy, walking upstairs to Suzy's room, smoking pot, and then having sex, all while mom is out playing tennis. A video called *Drugs in Black and White* talks about some of these same issues. It examines drug use and our perceptions of who is actually using, dealing, and/or buying drugs.

Music seems to mirror our beliefs. Two different perspectives about two different neighborhoods are offered below—can you relate to either one? Do you live in one of these neighborhoods now? The first neighborhood I would like to introduce you to is written in a song by The Offspring called "The Kids Aren't Alright." The lyrics begin by talking about how things were when they grew up. Kids had bright futures, goals, dreams and aspirations. But now the neighborhood has changed. Kids are dropping out of school, smoking pot, getting pregnant, overdosing on drugs and so on…

"What the hell is going on, the cruelest dream, reality
Chances thrown, nothing's free.
Longing for what used to be, still it's hard to see fragile lives shattered dreams."

"The Kids Aren't Alright"
The Offspring

Does this suggest to you many of our middle-class, suburban communities?

The second neighborhood I want to introduce you to is depicted in a song written by Nelly, called "Nellyville." The song is about utopia. Everyone is "livin' large," with jewels, cars, and money. When you look behind the material wealth you find what really matters in Nellyville:

> *"It's not game, it's a beautiful thang*
> *Imagine blocks and blocks of no cocaine, blocks with no gunplay.*
> *Ain't nobody shot, so ain't no news that day."*

> "Nellyville"
> Nelly

Do you think this represents many of our urban neighborhoods? Would you like to live in a community where you hear gunshots at night? Do you think your perspective might be a little bit different if you did? I know that there are kids and adults who sit in their rooms at night hoping, wishing, and praying for the same utopia Nelly talks about in his song. I am wishing for no news tonight as well.

Music offers the opportunity for many people to be heard without having to say a thing. Unlike radio talk shows and television shows, music offers a forum for those who do not have a voice. From the rap star singing about life on the streets to the rock star singing about alienation, these artists give kids a way to feel validated that their voices are being heard as well. Kids will express themselves one way or another, whether adults want to listen to the message or not.

29

Helping Dads Stay Involved

I was fortunate enough to have been brought up by both parents who have been married now for more than 50 years. There is no denying that they had help in raising me. Grandparents, siblings, aunts, uncles, cousins, and friends all had their hands in it. Like many other teenagers who grew up in the late 60s and early 70s, there were challenges put before us that we had to face and overcome. I had many healthy adults in my life while I was growing up, and I needed each and every one of them. I agree that most teens will go to other teens to talk about personal problems in their lives, but I also know that many of them end up talking with their parents, or another adult that they trust, to make sure that they are on the right track.

I have worked with many single parents who truly get a bad rap. I applaud those single parents who are trying to surround their child with other healthy adults. I applaud single moms and dads, because the work that goes into raising kids is incredible and single parents always have to be "on." I cannot imagine raising kids on my own. I know that many single parents today did not plan to raise their kids on their own; things happened that put them in that position. I also know there are adults who do choose to raise kids on their own, for a variety of reasons.

I have talked to many single moms who share stories of their ex-husbands who leave for a variety of reasons and do not stay connected to their kids. This is also true for the growing number of single dads whose wives leave them. We just don't hear about that happening as much, but it is a growing concern. I used to do a program called "Donuts for Dads," where dads would come share some sweets with their kids and then hear a workshop. It was the kids who got their dads to come. This workshop was called "Dads, Do You Know...?" and asked the following questions:

- Can you name your child's teacher or teachers?

- Can you name your child's favorite song, band, rapper or TV show?

- Do you know your child's favorite color, shoe size, or clothing size?

- Have you been to a teacher conference in the last six months?

- Have you been to a PTA meeting in the last six months?

At this particular workshop, about 75 dads showed up, from all different backgrounds and ethnicities. The kids left and we began our 15-minute conversation that lasted for almost an hour. Some of the fathers were married, but many were not. Story after story, they talked about custody issues, visitation rights, coping with the loss of a job, money issues, and still I got the message loud and clear: most of them had a strong sense of commitment to their kids. I have come into contact with dads from all walks of life, and each time I meet with them, I gather a little bit more wisdom. Here is a to-do list for dads:

- Agree upon rules, responsibilities, and discipline with your wife early on. Both parents must guide the child.

- Show what respect means. Walk what you talk.

- Be an attentive listener.

- Raise your child with strong morals and values.

- Do not set expectations for your kids before you set them for yourself.

- Tell your children stories about your childhood.

- Play outside, limit inside time.

- Get involved with a new baby, i.e. changing, feeding and diapering.

- Be there for your wife.

- Be consistent. Show up when you say you are going to show up.

- Praise your kids.

- Keep a journal of yourself that can be passed on to your kids.

- Have family rituals.

- Stand by your children even in a divorce.

- Learn patience and show love.

- Attend parent conferences and get involved in your kids' schools.

- Show your child that you love your mother.

- Do not be afraid of being affectionate with your son or daughter.

- Practice problem-solving in a peaceful manner.

- Read to your children, and have them read to you.

- Encourage your kids to do their best, even when they are tired of trying.

- Love your child in deed and truth.

- Spend more time than money on your child.

- Force yourself to find out something important in your child's life every single day.

- Provide a safe environment for your children.

- Have a strong spiritual/religious foundation.

- Have fun with your kids.

- Whether you are the biological father, stepfather, or single father, love your kids.

A colleague of mine and I were invited to spend the day observing conflict resolution training with 20 teenagers who were in jail awaiting adult prison. It was a very powerful day. I had the opportunity to speak with several of the young men who shared their stories. The common denominator throughout the young men was the fact that most of them grew up without their fathers or other significant healthy male role models playing an active role in their lives. Loving your kids is one thing, being an active participant is another. It is not enough to have dad in the house, around the house or next door to the house. What really matters is the quality of the relationship that dad develops with his son or daughter.

30

What It Means to Be a Parent

Many of you feel that music and its lyrics have an impact on what kids think, feel, say, or do. I agree with you. The argument made from both sides of the fence is well documented. Would I allow my 6-year-old son to hear lyrics full of profanity, violence, and sexuality? Of course not, nor would I show him an inappropriate G-rated movie if I felt the themes were too mature. That is my decision to make. We have control over what we bring into our own homes. But when my son and I walk out the door on a Monday morning, and I walk him down to the bus stop and wait with him, I know I have to let go. I have no control over what he sees and hears as the bus pulls away. Anybody reading this book can relate to what I am saying. Whether your child is 6 or 16, the same rule applies. We have control only over the decisions we make and what we allow into our environment.

A friend and neighbor of mine compared listening to music to drug addiction. Her concern is that many kids may begin harmlessly listening to pop radio or some kind of mainstream music, and then gradually move into a genre of music that may have messages that are negative and hostile. Once they become enmeshed in the subculture, it may be difficult to bring them out. As I stated earlier, there is a difference between listening and living your music. Most kids can listen to a particular song and are able to separate what the song is saying from how it relates to their lives. Some cannot, and internalize these messages to be truth. Others have these beliefs to begin with, and the music validates what they are thinking and feeling. Every child has many pages and chapters to his life. Some find it difficult to turn the page, others never move on to the next chapter. My goal in writing this book was to take an objective look at the role that music plays in kids' lives and to increase your level of awareness, along with offering you some strategies to put in your tool box. My personal goal is to continue to help, support, and encourage those kids and adults to turn the page and move on to the next chapter. I do believe I have learned more from kids in the last 20 years than they could have possibly learned from me, and I still have a lot more to learn. The one thing that seems to remain constant through it all is what a parent's job is supposed to be. I ask parents all the time if they had to write a job description for themselves, what would it look like? Would it include things like keeping your nose in your kids' business? What about just spending time with your kids? Would those two things be at the top of your list? I was talking to a group of parents during the early 90s when that question was posed to me. What would my job description look like? I did not have children at the time, so I took a guess. Here is how I responded:

Parents

One day late a curious question came to mind.
a question of innocence, a question of time.
The same question came to my friend Mr. Eek.
A question of urgency, a question of rhyme.

How could we not know—where could we find
the answer to the question that has been on our minds.
We'll go to Mr. Owl, he is sure to know the way—
He has seen all kinds, he understands the day.

*"Mr. Owl! Mr. Owl! Help us on our way, this important
question has interrupted our day!"*

*"Go to Miss Webster she knows all, look thru
her pages, walk down her halls."*

So off we went on this journey for a day.
A journey filled with riddle, a journey filled with haze.

*"Miss Webster! Miss Webster! Help us on our way,
this important question has interrupted our day!"*

Miss Webster sat silent as pages began to turn,
"Here is what you want, here is your concern,
"One that begets or brings forth offspring."

"That's it! That's it! We screamed in awe
This can't be it, it won't be, and it mustn't be all.
There must be a book, a guide, a How-To for all to see..."
We walked away silently, we walked away teased.

Mr. Eek looked gently over to me,
puzzled eyes, moving slow, looking to see,
where is the answer? What is to be?

I looked for strength, I looked for peace.
I looked for answers, I looked for relief.
Mr. Owl and Miss Webster they didn't know
Maybe its something you go through,
Not something you're told.

That's it! That's it! No wonder we didn't
know, its something you go through,
Not something you're told!

It's based on instinct through all the years.
It's based on love, honesty, and trust
It's not based on fears.
It's based on communication, beliefs and respect most of all.
All must be there, or else it will break down and fall.

"Well Mr. Eek, I think we figured it out
whether there is one or two in the house, it matters not
As long as the rest is all there
A parent's job is to really care."

One day or was it night, Mr. Eek looked
at me and asked *"What is a parent for?"*
"Don't ask me," I replied, *"I've never been one before!"*

Parenting is the most difficult and rewarding job one could ever have. Most parents tell me they would not trade it for anything in the world. I agree.

I hear the same thing from so many teachers about to retire who have loved what they do. They wouldn't trade their teaching career for anything in the world. I wrote this poem with the help of my wife who is truly an inspiration to everything that I do. Please share this poem with any educator you know. (Read the poem to the tune of "Yesterday," by the Beatles.)

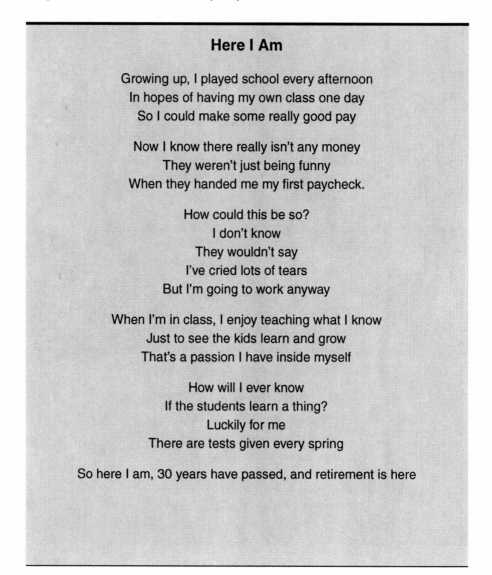

Here I Am

Growing up, I played school every afternoon
In hopes of having my own class one day
So I could make some really good pay

Now I know there really isn't any money
They weren't just being funny
When they handed me my first paycheck.

How could this be so?
I don't know
They wouldn't say
I've cried lots of tears
But I'm going to work anyway

When I'm in class, I enjoy teaching what I know
Just to see the kids learn and grow
That's a passion I have inside myself

How will I ever know
If the students learn a thing?
Luckily for me
There are tests given every spring

So here I am, 30 years have passed, and retirement is here

No way not me, perhaps next year
I still have lessons I need to share
I still have lessons I need to share

For those who give everything they have and were never told
Thank you.

And finally for the youth of today, I leave some thoughts from a leadership conference with 100 high school students. Please share this with your adolescents and teens, if you feel comfortable doing so.

Power In You

If you were told you could change the world, would you?
If you were told you could lead the way, could you?
If you were told you are the difference, would you believe it to be true?
You must believe in yourself always to have the
power in you.

Conclusion

We have come to the end of the song, but not the end of the record. The music that kids listen to will continue to change, reshape, and reform, but the essence of the messages music brings, both positive and negative, will remain the same. Most kids can differentiate between fantasy and reality, and most will listen to the music and take what they want and need from it. But for those young people who become enmeshed in its culture and fall prey to the music or artist that has the power to influence, we must all be vigilant in knowing and understanding their needs. From The Who's song "My Generation" to Slipknot's song "Surfacing," music is a reflection of the changing times. So much of music today is shunned by adults who either do not understand or cannot begin to relate to it, but as long as we have teenagers out there who will listen, we will have rock 'n roll. Please turn it up.

I hope this book has given you a glimpse of kids today and some of the issues they face, some of the same issues we all face. I hope you found some of the prevention strategies helpful, and you use the questions and comments as conversations within your own families. I hope you have a little more insight into what educators face today, and I hope that educators realize most parents are on their side. I hope you walk away from this book with a sense of hope and faith that our kids are going to be okay and that many of them are doing just fine, but that we still have work to do. I would really appreciate any feedback you may have regarding topics we talked about or those we did not have a chance to get to. Whenever I read a parenting book or a book in the self-help field, or attend a workshop, training or seminar, I always look for that one point, that one highlight that speaks to me that I can use right away to help someone else or use for my own insight. I hope you found yours.

Use music as a tool to discuss the challenges kids face today. Understand that many artists reflect a part of society that most adults do not want to talk about, but kids want to hear and learn about. Learn with them, but help them understand that there may be certain types of music that have no place in your home because the themes they represent are in conflict with your code of ethics. In a perfect world, a parent's code of ethics with regard to values would be similar in content to his neighbor's code of ethics, but we are not in a perfect world. Please remember to let your kids play and dance. Thank you for allowing me the opportunity to have this conversation with you, so until our next conversation begins…

As the Brotherhood of Man sang many years ago:

"United we stand, divided we fall,
and if our backs should ever be against the wall,
we will stand together, you and I."

Afterword

I believe it was 1991 that *Silence of the Lambs* was nominated for best picture and I can't remember if it won the Oscar. I do remember that it was nominated for its outstanding acting and storytelling, which makes me think that many adults have an interesting way of rationalizing, justifying and defending to others what they watch, listen to and read. Teenagers would say that adults who enjoy material with gratuitous sex and violence are hypocrites, because these same adults criticize their taste in music. Teenagers use the same argument when talking about adults who drink alcohol and tell teens not to drink.

I am not saying that *Silence of the Lambs* was not an excellent movie for those who enjoy that type of entertainment. But if you stop to think about it, it was a movie about a guy who eats people. It featured gratuitous violence, the same kind of violence that can be found in hundreds of songs—songs like "Mama's Gotta Die Tonight" (by Body Count), which tells the story of a son who believes his mother is racist, kills her by cutting her up in little pieces and sending her throughout the country in bags. Teenagers tell me that the song represents a fantasy the son has about killing his mother over her racist attitudes towards the son's girlfriend and people in general. Another song, "Timothy" (by the Buoys), came out in the 70s, and was widely criticized for lyrics that talked about cannibalism. In those days, it was the first pop hit of its kind to reach the top 40.

As adults, we can choose to listen to and watch whatever we want, but it's important to know that our behaviors influence our children. I include myself when I say this, because I listen to, watch, and read material that may be offensive to some. Like you, however, I will not expose my kids to things I find inappropriate. Many parents allowed their teens to watch *Silence of the Lambs* and others did not. That is the dilemma we face: there is no real agreement about what material is offensive to kids under the age of 17.

Movies that feature Freddy, Jason, and Chucky, slasher movies and cult movies such as *I Spit on Your Grave*, all seem to have several of the same features:

- Good vs. evil

- Gratuitous violence

- Usually a strong female victim (How many television shows, movies or comic books have a strong female hero in the lead role?)

- Sexual messages (The kids who die first usually are the ones having sex.)

- Absent or poor role models as parents

- Villain has psychological problems

- Villain dies and returns again and again

Could an expert who studies these movies come up with some social value, some reasons we need to have them as part of our culture? Could an expert tell us the psychological profile of the person who watches these movies and why? Does it really matter?

If a book tells a good story that we can relate to, if the movie has a message buried somewhere beneath its plot and if the song relates to us in a way we understand, do the actual contents matter?

It is up to us to decide what we are going to allow and support our children to do. If we give them money, we need to ask ourselves if they are spending it on age-appropriate movies, music and video games. It is also up to us, as parents, to be conscious of what we bring into our homes and expose our children to. It is our decision to make.

Appendix A
A Look at the Future

If I told you that only 300 of the past 3,500 years were without war, would that make you take another look at violence in the media? (*Violence and Your Child*, Arnold Arnold, Award Books, 1969)

If I told you that children living in two-parent families, who have a fair to poor relationship with their fathers, are at 68 percent higher risk to use alcohol, tobacco, or other drugs, compared to all teens living in two-parent homes, would you fathers spend more time with your kids? (National Center on Addiction and Substance Abuse at Columbia University (CASA), Survey, 1999)

Did you know that, in 1964, the *Ladies Home Journal* estimated that the average American child between the ages 5 and 14 witnessed the violent destruction of 13,000 human beings on television. In 1992, the Center for Media and Public Affairs found that, after viewing just 18 hours of television, children witnessed 1,846 acts of violence. (*TV Guide*, August 12, 1992)

What would life be like for our children's children's children if all of us stopped doing prevention in this country? Let's look at the statistics for the year 2090:

- Eighty percent of all kids smoke pot, since drug use has been legalized in 2050.

- Eighty-five percent of all kids age 13 drink alcohol three times a week.

- Sixty-two percent of all children are involved in a gang.

- Ninety-one percent of all children spend four hours a day at the computer.

- Seventy-four percent of all children are in therapy, due to the longer school day that starts at 6:30 A.M. and ends at 7:00 P.M., six days a week.

- Eighty percent of all educators are in therapy as well, due to longer school days and no pay increases since the year 2020.

- Thirty-four percent of all twelve-year-old kids are sexually active.

Of course there is another way to look at these numbers:

- Three percent of kids smoke pot due to adult intolerance to the drug.

- Four percent of kid's aged 17 drink alcohol as all adults and business that serve alcohol clamp down on underage drinking.

- Two percent of kids join gangs. Kids no longer have the need to belong because their families provide what they need. In the year 2020, community and school policies become one in addressing gang activity.

- Due to increased parental involvement and support, only ten percent of kids and educators need therapy, but they go together in hopes of working out the few problems they have.

- Two percent of 12-year-old kids are sexually active. Without all the exposure, no access to drugs, strong family units and strong neighborhood and community norms, it just doesn't enter their minds.

Utopia, maybe, but for our kids' sake, let's have a little optimism. We have 86 years to work on our strategic plan, so let's get started.

Appendix B
Eye-Opening Activity

Take out a piece of paper and write the names of all the bands you listened to when you were growing up. Write what was happening in our country and around the world during the same time period. See if political and social factors influenced the type of music and their lyrics. Usually the decade or two before lays the foundation for the decade to come. For example, the sexual revolution did not just materialize in the 60s—it resulted from events taking place during the late 40s and 50s. Following is a brief list of bands and artists (starting in the 50s) that have ended up on someone's "list" due to inappropriate themes, language, image or content.

1950s. Most artists from the 50s who appeared to play anything close to blues, who shook their body parts or who suggested that kids should be different from their parents, including Elvis Presley, Buddy Holly, Chuck Berry and Little Richard. (Most kids embraced these artists and most parents did not. Do you think this decade opened the door for things to come?)

1960s. Beatles, Stones, MC5, Frank Zappa, most bands out of San Francisco and many other 60s bands, because of lyrics pertaining to sex, drugs and anti-establishment messages.

1970s. Black Sabbath, Judas Priest, Kiss, Iron Maiden Grand Funk, Led Zeppelin, ACDC, and most rock to metal bands.

1970s into the 1980s. Slayer, Venom, Sex pistols, Misfits, Twisted Sister, Donna Summer, and others that used profane, sexual, violent, rebellious or satanic messages.

1980s into the 1990s. Metallica, Guns and Roses, Megadeth, Nine Inch Nails, Jane's Addiction, Marilyn Manson, Nirvana, NWA, Slayer, rap artists like Ice T, Ice Cube and most grunge bands like Pearl Jam and Alice in Chains.

1990s into 2004 and beyond. ICP, Korn, several rap and black metal artists, bands that represent hate, and several pop artists who are more provocative in person than their songs.

Many times parents hear about a particular band through their faith community, on television, in print material or will see a CD lying around the house. There are parents who only allow their children to listen to faith-based music, and have very strong opinions about music today. Some parents who talk with me about music have not actually listened to it, nor do they know anything about the artist. If they hear that the music has sexual, violent, or anti-faith messages or if the band's concerts are inappropriate, they include those performers on their lists of unacceptable music. If your code of ethics is faith-based, most (but not all) secular music would be off limits.

If you want to begin a conversation with your teen, think about asking him to make a list of his own? For many teens, this is a risk because you may not know what he is listening to. This activity can be a risk for you as well, because it can lead to conversations that you may not be prepared to have. Know the risks before you move ahead. I would encourage you to have this conversation, agreeing not to tear up posters or throw out CDs. Realize that you are *not* having this conversation to set up a power struggle with your teen. Once the rules are agreed to by both you and your teenager, share your lists and the themes the music and lyrics are trying to convey to the listener. Talk about culture and social norms as it relates to the music.

Appendix C
Prevention Plan for Educators

Every school is required to have a crisis plan, but it also makes sense to have a prevention plan in place as well. Several years ago I was asked to pull together a committee of youth, parents and educators, to develop a prevention plan schools could use as a framework.

Recommendation #1—Code of Ethics

In Hal Burbach's article, "Violence and Public Schools," one of the initiatives suggested is "*work to build a strong positive ethos in schools.*" During Search Institute's Midwest Forum, one topic was the erosion of values among youth. Ball State University researchers Barbara Larson and Diane Danne found that "*Forty-three percent of 12- to 18-year-olds say it's okay for siblings of either sex to hit each other as a way of dealing with conflict. Not only is there no strong taboo against violence, but it can also easily become a mark of honor in some youth subcultures.*"

A code of ethics is not rooted in policy, but in philosophy and absolute value. Development of the code of ethics should be a collaborative effort of youth, community and school faculty so all stakeholders' values are reflected in the code. The code can be displayed for everyone to see.

Recommendation #2—Violence Prevention Programs/Strategies

1. *Conflict Resolution/Life Skills*

   At a recent health conference, psychologist W. Rodney Hammond, Ph.D. of the Centers for Disease Control outlined what research suggests is most effective in preventing violence:

   • Make the program comprehensive by involving families, schools, and communities.

   • Launch anti-violence curricula in the primary grades and reinforce it across grade levels.

- Build personal and social assets that inoculate children against violent habits and diffuse their tendency to lash out physically when angry.

- Make the program content relevant to culture and ethnicity.

- Ultimately the most effective technique is the use of programs that develop students' violence-resistance skills.

Research into many of these violence programs indicates changes in knowledge and attitudes by those who use them. However, these programs must be used as they were intended. Infusion of programs may be successful, but come under more stringent guidelines for evaluation than do other programs. By looking at your schools' discipline incident and action codes, you will be able to develop strategies based on the specific needs of your school's population. Conflict Resolution and Peer Mediation programs, along with peace tables and classroom meetings, have an abundance of research that shows great effectiveness when used as part of a comprehensive prevention plan. (For more on research based programs, visit www.samhsa.gov).

2. *Mentoring Programs*

A senior involved in prevention-based programs, including Peer Helpers, for the last six years writes: *"I had the opportunity to speak to 5th graders at a local elementary school on the effects of ATOD. This experience impacted me in many ways. Most importantly, I discovered that I want to become a teacher. One kid looked to me and said, 'When I get into high school, I want to be like you.' I then realized that if I could touch one kid in one way and maybe give him a positive role model, imagine how many kids I would be able to touch in 30 years of teaching."*

Most researchers document low attachment as a precursor to ATOD, violence, and/or suicide. In Gavin DeBecker's book *The Gift of Fear*, DeBecker suggests that one of the leading precursors of attention-getting violent acts is being ignored or not feeling connected. Establishing mentoring programs that utilize community and high school leaders—working with younger children—has been found effective in providing children a sense of attachment. Once a child feels connected, academic success may increase. Search Institute lists 40 developmental assets, adult role models, and positive peer influence as asset-building characteristics every child needs to feel successful.

3. *After-School Programs*

The key to after-school programs is surveying students to determine what activities they would like to participate in during the hours following school. Research strongly suggests that ATOD use and other unhealthy behaviors (including violent and delinquent behavior) take place between the hours of 4:00 and 8:00 P.M. and before school starts. This research suggests that we must offer alternative activities for students and enable them to feel successful in areas other than academics. Remember that after-school programs do not need to be housed at the school building itself. Community and business leader involvement is essential in implementing a successful after-school program.

Recommendation #3—Staff Development

• *Team Building.* It is important for school faculty to support one another during the school year. This sense of family and attachment to school will create a team approach and a more positive climate.

• *Program Training.* In the 1993 article, "Comprehensive Steps Used to Stem Youth Violence" (*Education Week*), the author states that "*violence-prevention strategies should be taught in schools and to teachers, administrators, school staff members and health professionals who work with children.*" Whatever strategy is used, faculty should be trained and support the initiative. Programs that are not supported or are one-person-driven are more apt to fail.

• *Signs and Symptoms.* All educators need to be periodically updated on the symptoms and signs of child abuse, substance abuse and suicide. "*Children who are physically abused at home are much more likely to act out in violent and aggressive ways by the time they enter kindergarten.*" (*Science News*, January 12, 1991) Paul Mones states in his book, *When a Child Kills*, "*the most single reliable pre-incident indicator of parricide killing is child abuse.*"

• *Anger Management and Empathy.* In DeBecker's book *The Gift of Fear*, he cites that a "*predictor of violence is chronic anger in childhood.*" In Daniel Goldman's thought-provoking book, *Emotional Intelligence*, he describes seven key abilities most beneficial for human beings. Five of them have to do with learning the necessary tools to deal with anger and empathy. Lack of impulse control, lack of empathy, and inability to express feeling have all been documented as possible precursors to violent behavior. It is important for staff to be able to identify students who fit into some of these categories.

School-Wide Assistance Group (SWAG), Care Teams/Core Groups. Care teams are different from School-Wide Assistance Groups in that they deal specifically with the emotional and behavior needs of the child. These teams should be made up of teachers, school psychologists, social workers, counselors, and administrators. (For more information on Student Assistance programs check out www.sapaofga.org)

- *Drug Perception and Attitude.* It is important to understand the correlation between drugs and violence in terms of risk and protective factors. Training in drug use for educators, especially on the middle- and high-school level, is essential.

- *School Asset Mapping.* The focus has always been on the problem and how to fix it—needs assessments are limited in that they only point out what is needed. United Way developed a definition of asset mapping: *"members share skills and experiences that strengthen and develop each other's gifts."* Faculty members' gifts can be inventoried and used to develop a systematic plan for working together to better serve youth.

- *Safety and Security In-Services.* An in-service needs to address the "what if" questions. For example, *"What would I do if Johnny pulled a gun in my class?"* This in-service would also address issues concerning personal safety.

- *Staff Development Course.* Staff development and in-service is a challenge when staff members already have too much on their plates. Some options are:

  - *A staff development course* that trains staff in specific programs and strategies. (Trainer of Trainers model).

  - *A staff development course* that introduces the educator to youth risk behavior and signs and symptoms on a variety of topics.

  - *Monthly staff in-services* focusing on topics related to youth drug use and violence.

Recommendation #4—Crisis Protocol

It is becoming more and more difficult to implement system-wide programs due to academic demands. A logical, efficient and productive way is to integrate: 1) research-based programs; 2) strategies based on research; 3) comprehensive data collecting; and 4) a youth leadership team (to include peer programs like peer helpers and mediators) that develops an action plan with the support of staff.

Have a suicide and homicide protocol and a bully policy that makes sense. Many states currently have bully policies in place.

Recommendation #5—Environment

In the 1997 book by Don Campbell, *The Mozart Effect*, he describes the power that music can have on our attitudes, feelings, and moods. Recent data suggests that music (especially Mozart) can increase math and science scores. When you combine environmental factors like music, lighting, space, and color, the overall climate becomes more conducive to learning.

Do you believe playing music on a school bus, or during class, could have an impact on student's behavior? What about playing it during lunch? I do believe that incorporating music into the school day is a strategy that costs little and can offer big returns. A special thanks to Bernadette Leite, Gail Marchant, Herb Goldstien, Ryan Cooper, Penny Warren, Gail Smith, Renee May, Harriet Swift, and Dr. C.N. Haisten for their time, energy and ideas in the development of this prevention plan.

Appendix D
Tips for Teens:
How to Help a Friend

Parents often ask me to talk about ways their teens can be helpful to friends in difficult situations. Please pass this on to your teen, if you feel comfortable doing so.

Part One: Preparation

1. Think about what you want to say.

2. Think about how your friend might respond.

3. Think about what you want from the conversation (the goal).

4. Include others to role-play with you, if necessary.

5. Think about possible outcomes.

6. Know what is appropriate to handle and what needs to be taken to an adult (i.e., suicidal ideation or threats, abuse, personal safety issues). Understand that, in matters concerning safety, confidentiality must be broken and you must tell an adult.

7. Go back to the first step as many times as you need to.

Part Two: The conversation

1. Pick a safe place to talk.

2. Pick a time that is convenient for you and your friend.

3. Ask open-ended questions. Ask questions or make statements that require the person to give you more information: "*You look a little down, how are things going?*" or "*We haven't gotten together lately, how are things at home?*"

4. Listen for facts and feeling words.

5. Try to restate what the person is saying: "*So you're telling me you're failing math and may not pass? How do you feel about that?*"

6. Your friend may not want any feedback, opinions or advice, and may want you to just listen. If that is the case, let him or her know you are available to talk more and offer some times you would be available to do that. Make sure you follow up.

7. **Planting seeds**—if it appears that your friend does want you to respond, you can ask questions or make statements such as: "*I don't know if this will work, but have you thought about trying…?* or "*I had a friend who was in the same situation, and here are some things she tried, but I am not sure if it will work for you.*" If your friend shares but is reluctant to brainstorm for solutions, you can ask questions like: "*What is going to happen if you fail math?*" or "*What do you think might happen if things don't change?*" It is important to let your friend come up with some of his or her own ideas; if this isn't possible, plant some seeds by asking the above questions. Sometimes when we give advice to friends, it could backfire and you might be blamed for the outcome.

8. If the issue falls into the category of personal safety, get an adult involved. Offer to go with your friend to see a counselor or to talk with parents or other adults you trust.

*Be a friend but know when to let go. Sometimes friends have to go their separate ways due to challenges like drug use. Listen, care about and love your friends, but if they choose not to get help or are unwilling to help themselves, get to an adult. Know that losing a friendship—no matter how difficult that can be—is much easier than losing a friend.

Appendix E

When your child or teen reports bullying behavior:

1. Let them know that they are not in trouble and acknowledge their courage with coming forward.

2. Let them know it is your job as a parent to protect them.

3. Find out from them how the teasing or bullying behavior is impacting them.

4. Ask if they have reported the bullying to any school staff or other adults.

5. Ask what they have done to try to stop the teasing or bullying behavior.

6. Find out where it took place, who was involved and when it happened.

7. Tell them you will need to contact the school if personal safety issues are involved. Let them know that their name will not be used unless there is no other way.

8. A safety plan would need to be set up if those concerns exist. (This plan is put in place during a conference at the school between administration and the family.)

9. Let them know that you will keep them informed all along the way.

10. Find out if they have any friends that you can talk with to get their perspective. You would only talk with them with your child's or teen's permission.

11. Ask them if they would like to speak to any other adults about the teasing or bullying behavior.

12. Ask them if a call to the parents of the person who is bullying would be helpful. (Only to be used if no imbalance of power exists.)

13. Ask if mediation would be helpful. (Only to be used if no imbalance of power exists and you will need both parties' permission.)

14. Let them know that the police may need to get involved depending on the situation.

When the school or a parent calls to inform you that your child is involved in bullying behavior:

1. Begin by asking your child how he\she is doing.

2. Ask them if they are aware that the school has contacted you about their behavior.

3. Question them about the reports you have been receiving from a variety of sources that states he\she is involved in inappropriate teasing and\or bullying behavior

4. If they deny the behavior, reiterate the seriousness of the reports.

5. See if they can define what inappropriate teasing and bullying behavior is. (Refer back to whatever your child's or teen's class or school expectations and common language are).

6. Let them know that this behavior goes against your code of ethics and the school's common language. It will not be tolerated.

7. Let them know that they can talk with other adults at the school, including the counselor, to address some of the concerns that have come up. If the inappropriate teasing or bullying behavior does not stop, then other consequences will occur.

8. Let them know that you are there for them and as a family will get through this.

9. Seek outside assistance as needed.

Please understand that **some kids who report that they are being bullied are also bullying others, and some kids who are being labeled as a bully may actually be getting picked on themselves. It is important to be open to all possibilities.

Appendix F

What's New on the Internet? *Cyberbullying.*

Patti Agatston, Ph.D.

Prevention/Intervention Center

Young people are at the forefront of changes in how we communicate based on today's new technology. They are much faster to adapt to the new technology than those of us with a few grey hairs. Instant messages, blogging on the internet, and text messaging on cell phones, are all ways that young people use to keep in touch. While this new technology can be more efficient and more fun, it can also lead to abuse without proper guidance and forethought. As a parent, it is both a challenge and an important responsibility to familiarize yourself with the ways that your child is communicating with others. It is also critical to set clear guidelines for responsible use of this technology.

Currently the media has reported many stories of young people using the internet or other mobile devices to bully or harass other students. Cyberbullying is a term used to describe such behavior. Here are some examples of cyberbullying:

- sending threatening or harassing e-mails or instant messages

- creating a website that belittles or ridicules another student

- taking unflattering or inappropriate digital pictures of another student without their permission and sharing it with others or posting it on an internet site

- stealing someone's password from their instant message or e-mail account and sending mean or humiliating messages to others

- tricking someone into sharing sensitive personal information while instant messaging and then forwarding that information to others

The feeling of anonymity that people feel while in cyberspace can contribute to people sending messages that they would never say to someone in person. What many students (and many adults) do not understand, however, is that they are never truly invisible when using the Internet. We still leave "footprints' when we are in the online world, and these can often be traced back to us. Parents need to label such behaviors as inappropriate and bullying behaviors and be clear that such behavior will lead to a loss of online privileges. In some instances such behaviors could even lead to criminal or civil prosecution.

The internet offers tremendous opportunity for creating a better world, but with such rapid advancements we must educate ourselves and empower our young people with the values, tools, and skills to make cyberspace a safe and productive place for all.

For additional information check out these informative websites:

www.netsmartz.org—fun and interactive lessons for children, teens, and parents on internets

www.isafe.org

www.cyberbully.org

Appendix G
Self Injury behavior (cutting)

Self injury has been around for many years. Like other teen issues it never got much press back in the 70s and 80s like it does today. Many musicians who played in punk bands in the late 70s would cut on themselves as part of their stage act. Today, many rock stars and movie stars are very open about their experiences with cutting. I cannot walk into a middle or high school without hearing about groups of kids that are cutting.

Fauazza and Rosenthal (1993) developed three categories to describe self injury:

1. Major Mutilation—Castration, amputation, and permanent disfigure.

2. Stereotypic self mutilation—Head banging, finger and arm biting, eyeball pressing and so on. (Autistic, psychotic, schizophrenic and tourette to name a few).

3. **Superficial or moderate—(common) this is what I see most of starting in 5th grade (few) through 12th grade.**

Some thoughts:

1. Many times it runs the cycle of cutting to eating disorder back to cutting, especially during the middle school years among girls.

2. Habit forming—(Unhealthy coping skill) Many researchers view self injury as addictive behavior. Many kids who cut will share that it is difficult for them to stop and they may need some counseling that can offer them strategies and support in their recovery.

3. Survival skill—Most of these kids do not want to kill themselves, so they cut to feel normal. The cutting becomes a distraction for the emotional pain they may be in. There are kids who cut on themselves because they are curious or their friends are encouraging them to try it. For some it is a

fad that passes quickly, and for others cutting is a **symptom** of something much larger that is going on in their life.

4.   Many of these kids become guilt or shame based depending on how long the cutting goes on.

• Many of these kids have poor coping skills. Many others are over achievers and perfectionists who get good grades, are popular and are well respected.

If you type the words self injury or cutting into any search engine you will find volumes of information and strategies on the topic. If you want to have a conversation with your teen about cutting, you could start by saying, "On today's talk show I heard teens talking about cutting themselves with a razor, do you know anybody that has tried to do that?" I realize that there are some topics we just do not want to bring up or talk about because some parents believe it might put thoughts into a young person's head that were not present to begin with. But with self injury being what it is today and being talked about on television, in movies and in music, it might be a conversation worth your time. As always that is your decision to make, but I would rather have parents talking to their teens about this before your kid's friends do.

Appendix H
Song References and Resources

- Arrested Development, "Mr. Wendal," Speech, (*3 Years, 5 Months, and 2 Days in the Life of...*), © 1992, Chrysalis Records, EMI Blackwood, Inc.

- The Beatles, "Why Don't We Do It In The Road," Lennon and McCartney, (*The White Album*), © 1968 World by Northern Songs Ltd., Apple Records Music Publishing.

- Brotherhood of Man, "United We Stand," 1970, Hiller and Simons

- Bob Dylan, "The Times They Are A Changin," © 1964 Columbia Records.

- Charlie Daniels, "Long Haired Country Boy," (*Fire on the Mountain*), © 1974 Kama Sutra Records.

- Lesley Gore, "It's My Party," © 1963 Mercury Records.

- Hatebreed, "You're Never Alone" (*Perseverance*), © 2002 Universal Records.

- Led Zeppelin, "The Lemon Song," Page, Plant, Jones, and Bonham (*Led Zeppelin II*), © 1969 Atlantic Recording Corp.

- Nelly, "Nellyville," © 2002 Universal Records.

- The Offspring, "The Kids Aren't Alright" *(Americana)*, © 1998 Underachiever Music.

- Suicidal Tendencies, "Can't You See it F***kin Hurts," Muir and George, (*Controlled By Hatred*), © 1989 CBS Records.

- Pink Floyd, "Another Brick in the Wall, Part II" (*The Wall*), Walters, © 1979 Walters, Pink Floyd Music Publishers, EMI Records.

- REM, "Everybody Hurts" (*Automatic for the People*), © 1993.

- Rush, "Dreamline," lyrics by Peart (*Roll the Bones*), © 1991 Atlantic.

- Warrior Soul, "The Losers," Clarke, Ricco and McClanahan, © 1987 Dead Government Music/Azias Music BMI.

- XTC, "Dear God," Partridge, © 1986 Virgin Records.

- Frank Zappa, "Bobby Brown," Zappa (*Sheik YerBouti*), © 1979 Frank Zappa.

Poem

- *BaBa Fats*, Shel Silverstein

Bullying

- Bully Beware, www.bullybeware

- School Bully on line, www.bullyonline.org

- No Bullying, www.nobully.org

- www.stopbullyingnow.hrsa.gov

Character Education

- Character Counts!, www.charactercounts.org

- The Character and Ethics Project, www.ethicsproject.org

Child Advocacy

- National Children's Coalition, www.child.net

Diversity and Tolerance

- Teaching Tolerance, www.teachingtolerance.com

Drug and Substance Abuse

- Drug Wars, www.drugwarfacts.org

- Survey on Drug Use, www.monitoringthefuture.org

- Drug Rehabilitation, www.orpartnership.com

- Alanon-Alateen Family Groups, www.al-anon-alateen.org

- Campaign for Tobacco-Free Kids, www.tobaccofreekids.org

- National Clearinghouse for Alcohol and Drug Information, www.health.org

Fatherhood

- Fathers World, www.fathersworld.com

- www.americasdadvocate.com

Mental Health

- Mental Health Matters, www.mental-health-matters.com

Mentoring

- National Mentoring Partnership, www.mentoring.org

- OJJDP Juvenile Mentoring Program, http://ojjdp.ncjrs.org/jump/index.html

Music

- Heavy Metal, www.metal-rules.com

- Progressive World, www.progressiveworld.net

- Rap and Hip-Hop Guide, www.Rap.about.com

- Rap Dictionary, www.rapdictionary.org

- Gothic—Dark side of the Net, www.darklinks.net

- Gang Slang, www.Gangsrus.com

Parenting and Parent Involvement

- Discipline and Behavior, www.disciplinehelp.com

- The Center for Effective Discipline, www.stophitting.com

- Girls and Boys Town Parenting, www.parenting.org

- National Coalition for Family Involvement in Education, www.ncpie.org

- National Youth Development Information Center, www.nydic.org

- National PTA www.pta.org

- Georgia PTA www.georgiapta.org

- www.elainegibson.net\parenting

Protective Factors for Youth

- Protective Factors, http://www.co.missoula.mt.us/measures/protective.htm

- Search Institute, www.searchinstitute.org

Safety

- Tips for Teacher's Safety, www.teachersworkshop.com

Violence Prevention

- Family Violence Prevention Fund, http://endabuse.org

- Institute for Community Peace, www.peacebeyondviolence.org

- National Crime Prevention Council, www.ncpc.org

- National Youth Network, www.usdoj.gov/kidspage/getinvolved

- National Youth Violence Prevention Resource Center, www.safeyouth.org

- Stop the Violence, www.stv.net

978-0-595-31220-7
0-595-31220-9

Printed in the United States
71773LV00005B/37-66